Homework Booklet

Fun with Math

Grade 4

By
Jan Kennedy

Cover Design by
Vickie Lane

Inside Illustrations by
Chris Olsen

Published by Instructional Fair • TS Denison
an imprint of

 **McGraw-Hill**
Children's Publishing

9 781568 226071

ABOUT THE AUTHOR

Jan Kennedy has earned degrees from the University of Dayton and Ohio State University. Jan is an experienced author and teacher dedicated to her profession and the children she teaches.

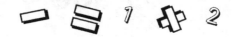

CREDITS:

Author: Jan Kennedy
Cover Design: Vickie Lane
Inside Illustrations: Chris Olsen
Project Director/Editor: Linda Kimble
Editors: Wendy Roh Jenks, Sharon Kirkwood
Typesetting/Layout: Pat Geasler
Cover Photos: © Image Club Graphics, © Digital Stock, © Corel Corporation, © Foto Rom, and © McGraw-Hill Children's Publishing

McGraw-Hill
Children's Publishing

A Division of The McGraw-Hill Companies

Published by Instructional Fair • TS Denison
An imprint of McGraw-Hill Children's Publishing
Copyright © 1998 McGraw-Hill Children's Publishing

Send all inquiries to:
McGraw-Hill Children's Publishing
3195 Wilson Drive NW
Grand Rapids, Michigan 49544

ISBN: 1-56822-607-1

Table of Contents

Answer Key (in middle of book)

 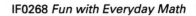

Salute to Sequencing

Study each sequence. Draw the next four logical pictures in the sequence.

1. ▣ , ⊡ , ⊡⊡ , _____

2. ⊛ , ⊛ , ⊛ , _____

3. •• , •••• , •••• , _____

4. ⊓• , ⊐•• , _____

5. ⬡ , ⟨8⟩ , ⬡ , ⟨9⟩ , _____

6. ⏜⏜⏜ , ⏜⏜⏜ , ⏜⏜⏜ , _____

7. #ˣ , #|ˣ , #|ˣ , #|ˣ , _____

8. ○ , ○ᓚ , ○ᓗ , ○ᓗ , _____

ook at the numbers in each flag. Read the rule, then
rite the next four numbers of the pattern.

rule-
+2,+4,
+6,+8

0,2,6,12,...

rule-
x2

7,14,28,56...

rule-
x2

2,4,8,16,...

rule-
+3,+5,+7

3,6,11,18,...

rule-
tens and
ones place
increase by
1 each time.

12,23,34,45...

rule-
+4,-1,
+4,-1

1,5,4,8,...

rule-
-12

96,84,72,60,...

rule-
x2,-2,
x2,-2

3,6,4,8,...

rule-
+8

48,56,64,72,...

onus —Extend the number patterns in each flag as far as
ou wish.

Round and Round

Round each number to the nearest . . .

ten.   57 ____   85 ____   77 ____   97 ____

42 ____   16 ____   33 ____   45 ____

hundred.   116 _____   784 _____   345 _____

571 _____   901 _____   650 _____

350 _____   446 _____   891 _____

thousand.   3,783 _____   2,520 _____

4,015 _____   7,500 _____

2,067 _____   4,474 _____

1,814 _____   6,642 _____

5,789 _____   8,417 _____

Round the approximate distances between these cities to the nearest thousand.

	Miles	Nearest Thousand
Albany, NY to San Francisco, CA	3,146	_____
Albuquerque, NM to Boston, MA	2,220	_____
Hartford, CT to St. Louis, MO	1,079	_____

r. Watiz Yer Zip, the mathematical postman, uses city zip des to practice his rounding skills. Help him complete e chart.

Cities	Zip Codes	Round to Hundreds	Round to Thousands
Austin, TX	78711		
Salem, OR	97310		
Lansing, MI	48909		
Des Moines, IA	50309	50,300	
Juneau, AK	99811		
Sacramento, CA	95814		
Columbus, OH	43266		
Santa Fe, NM	87503		
Chicago, IL	60601		61,000
Atlanta, GA	30301		
Richmond, VA	23219		
St. Paul, MN	55101		
Honolulu, HI	96815		
Tallahassee, FL	32301		

Comparatively Speaking

Write the answer to each problem on the line. Then writ
<, >, or = in each box to compare the numbers.

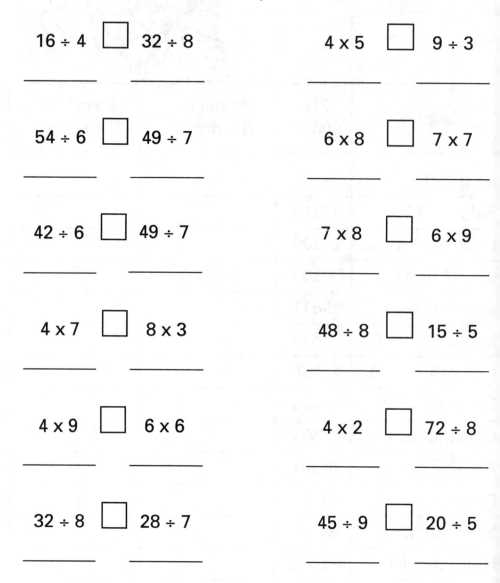

16 ÷ 4 ☐ 32 ÷ 8   4 x 5 ☐ 9 ÷ 3

_____ _____   _____ _____

54 ÷ 6 ☐ 49 ÷ 7   6 x 8 ☐ 7 x 7

_____ _____   _____ _____

42 ÷ 6 ☐ 49 ÷ 7   7 x 8 ☐ 6 x 9

_____ _____   _____ _____

4 x 7 ☐ 8 x 3   48 ÷ 8 ☐ 15 ÷ 5

_____ _____   _____ _____

4 x 9 ☐ 6 x 6   4 x 2 ☐ 72 ÷ 8

_____ _____   _____ _____

32 ÷ 8 ☐ 28 ÷ 7   45 ÷ 9 ☐ 20 ÷ 5

_____ _____   _____ _____

mpare these numbers by writing <, >, or = in each
cle. Then follow the directions below to discover the
thor of the book, *Tales of a Fourth Grade Nothing.*

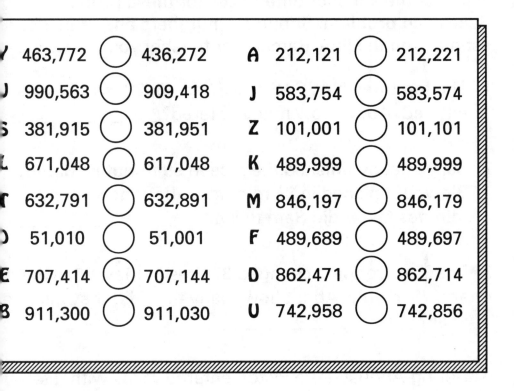

Y 463,772	◯	436,272	A 212,121	◯	212,221
J 990,563	◯	909,418	J 583,754	◯	583,574
S 381,915	◯	381,951	Z 101,001	◯	101,101
L 671,048	◯	617,048	K 489,999	◯	489,999
T 632,791	◯	632,891	M 846,197	◯	846,179
O 51,010	◯	51,001	F 489,689	◯	489,697
E 707,414	◯	707,144	D 862,471	◯	862,714
B 911,300	◯	911,030	U 742,958	◯	742,856

cord the letters of the problems with > as the answer.
en unscramble them to discover the author's name.

___ ___ ___ ___ ___   ___ ___ ___ ___ ___

Race Station Estimation

The famous race car driver, S. Tim Ate, needs your help t
estimate the sums or differences for these problems.
Read each problem. Round the numbers and write your
estimate on the line. Remember to label your answers.

1. The top three NASCAR races had 43, 28, and 24 cars
entered. About how many entered? _____

2. Sam Speedy finished the race in 58 minutes. Barney
Blowout finished in 84 minutes. About how many
minutes faster did Sam finish? _____

3. The Tire Troopers changed 37 tires in May, 65 in June,
and 73 in July. About how many tires did they change
in all? _____

4. During August, Pete Piston entered races with distances of 316, 450, and 287 miles. About how many
miles did Pete race in August? _____

5. This summer 89 cars were involved in crashes. Last
year, only 65 were involved in crashes. About how
many more crashed this summer? _____

6. In the last 5 years, the Indy 500 has had 33 cars race
each year. About how many cars raced during this
5-year period? _____

he kids who live near BJ's Fun Park were practicing for
e fall go-cart races. Round the numbers and estimate
e total number of laps each child practiced during the
ummer months. Then calculate the actual amount of
tal laps and average per month to the nearest lap.

Driver	Practice Laps			Estimate of Total Laps	Actual Total Laps	Average Laps Per Month
	June	July	Aug.			
Shelly	53	62	68	**180**	**183**	**61**
Andy	47	56	58			
Sydney	57	65	68			
Tyesha	57	65	68			
Toby	43	41	46			
Hannah	50	55	53			
Mika	46	52	48			
José	52	53	49			
Myra	48	37	51			
Kurt	61	58	53			
Morgan	68	74	69			
Cassandra	48	45	49			
Jordan	54	46	50			

What's the Difference?

Find the difference for each problem. Then write the letters to the corresponding answers on the lines below to solve the riddle.

1. $600.04
   $-$ 1.76
          A

2. $700.40
   $-$ 27.15
          S

3. $200.08
   $-$ 66.73

4. $500.00
   $-$320.60
          S

5. $101.10
   $-$ 64.92
          I

6. $301.00
   $-$214.16

7. $805.05
   $-$371.59
          I

8. $500.50
   $-$193.76
          S

9. $404.10
   $-$272.36

What kind of fish is a bargain?

50% OFF!

A ___ ___ ___ ___ ___ ___ ___ ___
$673.25 $598.28 $433.46 $131.74 $86.84 $36.18 $179.40 $133.3

⊕ 12 ◣

lve each problem. Shade answers that appear on the
ngo card. Then draw a line through the winning row.

1.	7,136 – 2,298	**2.**	8,430 – 2,554	**3.**	5,032 – 2,774
4.	3,002 – 1,596	**5.**	2,145 – 1,989	**6.**	7,818 – 5,446
7.	9,014 – 2,565	**8.**	4,141 – 2,067	**9.**	1,042 – 209
0.	8,612 – 4,754	**11.**	9,155 – 3,083	**12.**	4,313 – 2,246

B	I	N	G	O
,067	1,049	232	198	4,838
,776	1,406	1,492	383	6,903
,151	2,248	3,858	201	5,758
,372	5,858	1,440	833	1,150
,997	2,074	5,771	700	6,449

Missing Addends

The Number Muncher has been eliminating addends from these problems! Write the missing numbers in each square.

1. 5 3 ☐ ☐
  + 2 ☐ 7 8
  ———————
  8,0 3 2

2. 3 ☐ ☐ 6
  + 8 1 7 ☐
  ———————
  11,9 5 1

3. ☐ 3 ☐
  + 3 2 6 ☐
  ———————
  7,6 5 ☐

4. 2 5 ☐
   1 1 5
  + ☐ 7 8
  ———————
   9 5 0

5. 6 0 4
   ☐ ☐ 6
  + 6 7 ☐
  ———————
  2,0 3 8

6. ☐ 3 ☐
   3 4 7
  + 9 ☐ 4
  ———————
  2,1 1 6

7. 4 6 7 8
   2 ☐ 3 8
  + 1 5 ☐ ☐
  ———————
  8,4 3 5

8. 2 1 ☐ 6
   ☐ 3 4 9
  + 5 ☐ 2 5
  ———————
  11,1 5 0

9. 1 ☐ 4
   3 2 2 ☐
  + 2 ☐ 7
  ———————
  7,9 4 ☐

10. 5 ☐ 6 3
   ☐ 4 9 2
  + 7 7 7 ☐
  ———————
  22,2 3 4

11. ☐ 7 3 4
   2 ☐ 6 8
  + 5 6 6 ☐
  ———————
  18,1 7 0

12. 7 5 ☐ ☐
   3 9 9
  + 3 ☐ 7
  ———————
  15,2 3 ☐

⊕ 14 ▭

how off your addition skills by adding the numbers in
ese problems. Remember to place commas in the
swers. Then write the letters to the corresponding
swers on the lines below to solve the riddle.

1.   11,565
   + 89,248
         U

2.   32,176
   + 74,148
         N

3.   85,468
   + 18,527
         N

4.   7,427
     8,491
   + 5,565
         G

5.   9,462
     8,153
   + 3,976
         B

6.   3,666
     7,246
   + 9,819
         B

7.   4,877
     3,251
     9,464
   + 3,849
         U

8.   3,507
     9,884
     6,442
   + 1,746
         S

9.   7,659
     1,999
     8,324
   + 5,371
         Y

**What do you get if you cross
an insect and a rabbit?**

$\overline{,591}$ $\overline{100,813}$ $\overline{21,483}$ $\overline{21,579}$ $\overline{20,731}$ $\overline{21,441}$ $\overline{103,995}$ $\overline{106,324}$ $\overline{23,353}$

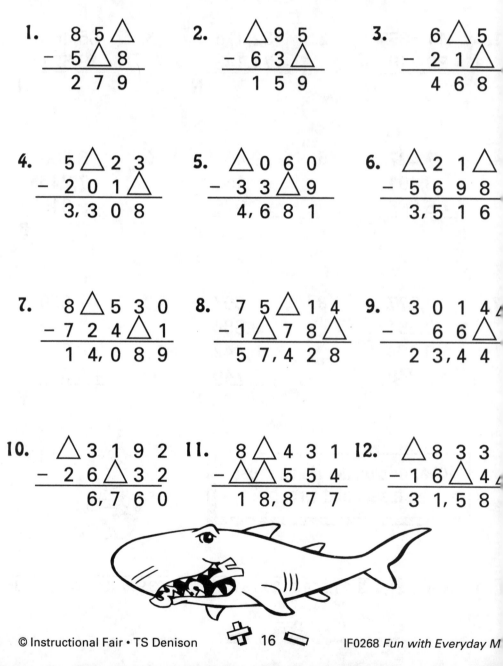

Get It Right

Take a bite out of subtraction. Donald Difference did that
Now it's up to you to put the "bites" back by writing the
missing digits for these subtraction problems.

1. 8 5 △
    – 5 △ 8
    ‾‾‾‾‾‾‾
    2 7 9

2. △ 9 5
    – 6 3 △
    ‾‾‾‾‾‾‾
    1 5 9

3. 6 △ 5
    – 2 1 △
    ‾‾‾‾‾‾‾
    4 6 8

4. 5 △ 2 3
    – 2 0 1 △
    ‾‾‾‾‾‾‾‾‾
    3, 3 0 8

5. △ 0 6 0
    – 3 3 △ 9
    ‾‾‾‾‾‾‾‾‾
    4, 6 8 1

6. △ 2 1 △
    – 5 6 9 8
    ‾‾‾‾‾‾‾‾‾
    3, 5 1 6

7. 8 △ 5 3 0
    – 7 2 4 △ 1
    ‾‾‾‾‾‾‾‾‾‾‾
    1 4, 0 8 9

8. 7 5 △ 1 4
    – 1 △ 7 8 △
    ‾‾‾‾‾‾‾‾‾‾‾
    5 7, 4 2 8

9. 3 0 1 4 △
    –   6 6 △
    ‾‾‾‾‾‾‾‾‾‾‾
      2 3, 4 4

10. △ 3 1 9 2
     – 2 6 △ 3 2
     ‾‾‾‾‾‾‾‾‾‾‾
       6, 7 6 0

11. 8 △ 4 3 1
     – △ △ 5 5 4
     ‾‾‾‾‾‾‾‾‾‾‾
     1 8, 8 7 7

12. △ 8 3 3
     – 1 6 △ 4 △
     ‾‾‾‾‾‾‾‾‾‾‾
     3 1, 5 8

▪mela Perfect would like you to check her math
▪oblems so she can get a perfect score. Check problems
▪ing addition and circle any incorrect problems.

Example:

```
          1 1
1,847    1,4̷9̷8
- 359   + 359
1,498    1,857
```

1.
```
  976
- 392
  584
```

2.
```
 1,892
-  566
 1,326
```

3.
```
 2,747
-1,283
 1,454
```

4.
```
 7,494
-5,688
 1,806
```

5.
```
 8,951
-2,497
 6,454
```

6.
```
 3,456
-2,891
   575
```

7.
```
 4,000
-2,674
 1,325
```

8.
```
 7,216
-4,588
 2,628
```

9.
```
 1,925
-  396
 1,671
```

Don't Be "Coin"fused!

Help the clerk determine your change. The most efficien
way to count change is to start with the cost of the item
and count to the amount of cash given. Draw the money
you would receive using the least amount of bills and
coins. Use these symbol: $5 $1 Ⓠ Ⓓ Ⓝ Ⓟ

Cost of Item	Amount Given	Your change is . . .
$2.97	$5.00	
$5.68	$10.00	
$14.27	$15.00	
$3.64	$5.00	
$10.68	$20.00	
$1.99	$5.00	
$16.75	$20.00	
$12.47	$15.00	

money

e the abbreviations in the Coin Box to list the number
coins and their denominations for the amount shown
each bank.

Coin Box	
HD =	50¢
Q =	25¢
D =	10¢
N =	5¢
P =	1¢

45¢
4 coins

_____ _____

_____

40¢
5 coins

_____ _____

51¢
5 coins

_____ _____

_____ _____

59¢
7 coins

_____ _____ _____

_____ _____

82¢
5 coins

_____ _____

_____ _____

42¢
6 coins

_____ _____

22¢
6 coins

_____ _____

76¢
4 coins

_____ _____

"Cent"sational Math

Solve the problems. Write the letters to the correspondir
answers on the lines below to solve the riddle.

1.
$$\begin{array}{r} \$17.84 \\ - \;\; 6.47 \\ \hline \end{array}$$
P

2.
$$\begin{array}{r} \$32.16 \\ - 27.88 \\ \hline \end{array}$$
I

3.
$$\begin{array}{r} \$21.16 \\ - 13.79 \\ \hline \end{array}$$
N

4.
$$\begin{array}{r} \$6.38 \\ + 5.37 \\ \hline \end{array}$$
E

5.
$$\begin{array}{r} \$21.48 \\ + \;\; 9.99 \\ \hline \end{array}$$
5

6.
$$\begin{array}{r} \$30.03 \\ - 19.46 \\ \hline \end{array}$$
E

7.
$$\begin{array}{r} \$14.60 \\ - 11.33 \\ \hline \end{array}$$
N

8.
$$\begin{array}{r} \$12.05 \\ - \;\; 9.98 \\ \hline \end{array}$$
S

9.
$$\begin{array}{r} \$15.69 \\ + 21.47 \\ \hline \end{array}$$
O

What has fifty heads and
fifty tails?

$\overline{}\;\overline{}$ $\overline{}\;\overline{}\;\overline{}\;\overline{}\;\overline{}\;\overline{}$
$31.47 $37.16 $11.37 $11.75 $7.37 $3.27 $4.28 $10.57 $2.07

makes good "cents" to understand math. Solve each oblem. Remember the dollar sign and decimal point.

$78.19	$85.36	$66.72	$59.81
+ 56.77	+ 27.74	+ 83.38	+ 72.19

$31.62	$81.33	$50.08	$90.10
− 19.44	− 59.97	− 34.69	− 45.38

$9.65	$6.39	$5.49	$8.28
x 7	x 9	x 6	x 8

5$\overline{)\$9.35}$ 8$\overline{)\$9.92}$ 7$\overline{)\$8.19}$ 3$\overline{)\$8.49}$

McFrogs and a Movie

Circle the place value of each underlined digit in the first column. Write the letters of the corresponding answers on the lines below to solve the riddle.

1. 176,3̲14	**I**	3,000	**H**	300	**P**	30,000
2. 48̲1,572	**E**	80,000	**D**	8,000	**O**	800,000
3. 9̲44,361	**A**	90,000	**E**	900,000	**K**	9,000
4. 278,9̲55	**M**	9,000	**G**	90	**L**	900
5. 383̲,159	**C**	3,000	**B**	30,000	**T**	300,000
6. 2̲75,413	**S**	200,000	**U**	20,000	**W**	2,000
7. 18̲8,045	**V**	8,000	**F**	80,000	**F**	800
8. 5̲06,721	**E**	50,000	**R**	5,000	**F**	500,000
9. 74̲7,090	**D**	400,000	**N**	40,000	**I**	4,000
10. 1̲16,949	**L**	1,000	**R**	100,000	**C**	100
11. 56̲2,826	**K**	6,000	**I**	60,000	**A**	600,000

What do frogs like to eat with their hamburgers?

___ ___ ___ ___ ___ ___
7   10   3   9   5   1

___ ___ ___ ___ ___
8   4   11   2   6

IF0268 Fun with Everyday M

Show the place value of the underlined digit by outlining each movie marquee according to the color code.

one thousands—*yellow* one millions—*purple*
ten thousands—*green* ten millions—*orange*
hundred thousands—*red* hundred millions—*blue*

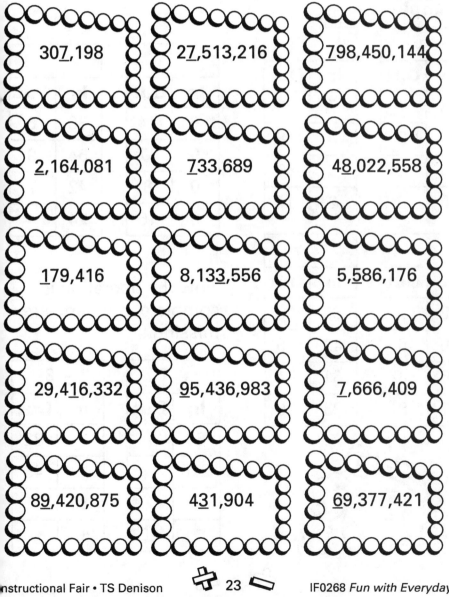

30<u>7</u>,198

2<u>7</u>,513,216

<u>7</u>98,450,144

<u>2</u>,164,081

<u>7</u>33,689

4<u>8</u>,022,558

<u>1</u>79,416

8,1<u>3</u>3,556

5,<u>5</u>86,176

29,4<u>1</u>6,332

<u>9</u>5,436,983

<u>7</u>,666,409

8<u>9</u>,420,875

4<u>3</u>1,904

<u>6</u>9,377,421

Math Operations

Dr. Math E. Matics, a famous surgeon, has performed many operations on his patients, but he has forgotten the "operations" for these math boxes. At the top of each chart write the math operation performed. The first one is done for you.

Example:

÷ 5	
In	**Out**
35	7
15	3
45	9
30	6

In	Out
7	49
4	28
9	63
2	14

In	Out
6	14
9	17
0	8
8	16

In	Out
36	6
54	9
42	7
24	4

In	Out
28	7
20	5
16	4
32	8

In	Out
36	29
42	35
61	54
23	16

Now the operation is complete, but parts are missing.

÷ 7	
In	**Out**
56	
210	
	7
	25

−18	
In	**Out**
	82
	48
30	
201	

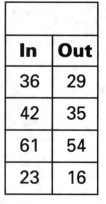

...lve the problems along each math pathway. Then write
...e letters to the corresponding answers on the lines be-
...w to solve the riddle.

$8 \times 6 \div 12 \times 6 \div 3 \times 4 - 13 =$ _____ C

$32 \div 4 \times 8 \div 8 \times 5 \div 10 \times 9 =$ _____ E

$48 \div 6 \times 5 \div 4 \times 16 \div 8 \div 4 =$ _____ P

$30 \div 5 \times 6 \div 36 \times 9 \times 8 + 6 =$ _____ I

$14 \times 2 \div 4 \times 12 \div 3 \times 2 - 4 =$ _____ D

$4 \times 10 \div 8 \times 15 \div 5 \div 3 \times 6 =$ _____ O

$63 \div 9 \times 6 \div 3 \div 2 \times 5 \div 5 =$ _____ C

$9 \times 4 \div 3 \times 2 \times 10 \div 8 \times 2 + 4 =$ _____ P

$16 \div 4 \times 8 \div 32 \times 8 \div 4 + 64 =$ _____ O

$2 \times 7 \div 7 \times 12 \div 2 \times 3 \div 6 =$ _____ L

**Why did the 4th grader make his
dad sit on top of the freezer?**

...e wanted an ___ ___ ___ ▬ ___ ___ ___ ___
      78 19 36   7 30 6 52

___ ___ ___
 5 66 64

Multiplication Mysteries

6	8	1
7	4	3
5	2	9

Use the Tic-Tac-Times board to write th[e]
correct number in each shape. Then
multiply to find each answer.

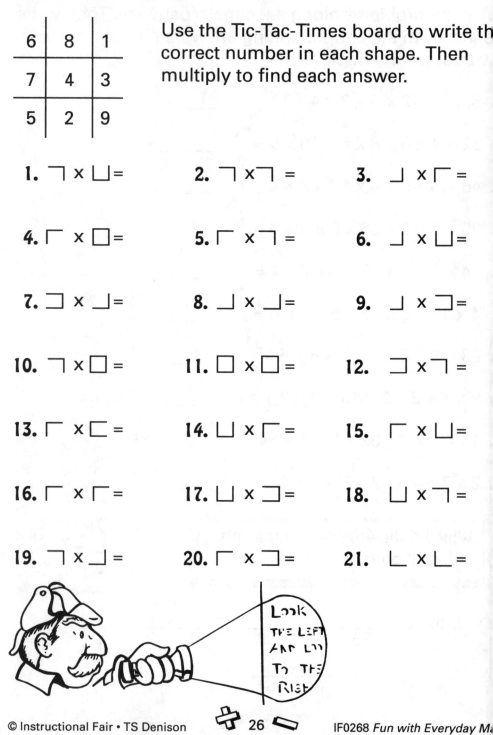

1. ⌐ × ⌎ =

2. ⌐ × ⌐ =

3. ⌏ × ⌌ =

4. ⌌ × □ =

5. ⌌ × ⌐ =

6. ⌏ × ⌎ =

7. ⌐ × ⌏ =

8. ⌏ × ⌏ =

9. ⌏ × ⌐ =

10. ⌐ × □ =

11. □ × □ =

12. ⌐ × ⌐ =

13. ⌌ × ⌊ =

14. ⌎ × ⌌ =

15. ⌌ × ⌎ =

16. ⌌ × ⌌ =

17. ⌎ × ⌐ =

18. ⌎ × ⌐ =

19. ⌐ × ⌏ =

20. ⌌ × ⌐ =

21. ⌊ × ⌊ =

Look
THE LEFT
AND UP
To THE
RIGHT

nd the products. Then circle each problem in the grid.
oblems will be found vertically, horizontally, or
agonally.

6 x 5 = _____	9 x 8 = _____	0 x 4 = _____
7 x 7 = _____	8 x 3 = _____	5 x 8 = _____
4 x 8 = _____	6 x 7 = _____	6 x 4 = _____
3 x 9 = _____	4 x 4 = _____	8 x 7 = _____
8 x 8 = _____	9 x 9 = _____	5 x 7 = _____
7 x 3 = _____	6 x 9 = _____	6 x 8 = _____
5 x 5 = _____	6 x 6 = _____	9 x 7 = _____

2	6	14	18	42	4	10	7	18	5	5	25	12	8	0
1	8	8	64	10	4	12	7	49	6	7	42	1	3	9
3	5	29	44	4	5	25	49	9	20	24	45	3	24	8
8	7	0	36	40	32	90	54	4	3	9	27	0	27	7
7	8	4	48	23	63	9	7	4	9	58	9	2	70	5
56	3	0	9	5	8	40	6	6	36	80	5	81	8	16
4	2	63	26	10	38	3	5	14	4	8	35	2	12	6
7	3	21	15	2	32	16	30	1	81	24	20	6	2	6
1	9	72	12	8	44	25	24	18	48	6	8	48	3	4
81	8	54	4	52	40	5	7	35	6	60	5	15	4	4
9	49	1	63	32	4	6	28	2	3	4	10	16	2	8

Master Multiplication

Compute these multiplication problems. Write the letters
to the corresponding answers below to solve the riddle.

U
1. 38
   x 17

E
2. 66
   x 28

U
3. 2?
   x 5?

R
4. 39
   x 16

B
5. 47
   x 27

R
6. 2?
   x 9?

M
7. 76
   x 59

H
8. 63
   x 74

G
9. 2?
   x 9?

What do you get when you cross a
bee and chopped meat?

A ___ ___ ___ ___ ___   ___ ___ ___ ___
   4,662 1,682 4,484 1,269 646   624 2,548 1,848 1,98

Write the missing factors for these problems.

1.
```
  6 □
× 6
-----
4 0 8
```

2.
```
  □ 4
× 5
-----
1 7 0
```

3.
```
  2 □
× 8
-----
2 0 8
```

4.
```
  □ 6
× 5
-----
2 8 0
```

5.
```
  3 □ 4
× 8
-------
2 5 1 2
```

6.
```
  □ 4 5
× 3
-------
2 2 3 5
```

7.
```
  2 9 □
× 7
-------
2 0 8 6
```

8.
```
  1 1 □
× 4
-----
4 5 6
```

9.
```
  4 □ 9
× 5
-------
2 4 9 5
```

10.
```
  □ 2 3
× 9
-------
7 4 0 7
```

11.
```
  3 7 □
× 4
-------
1 5 0 8
```

12.
```
  2 0 □
× 7
-------
1 4 4 9
```

13.
```
  8 7 8
×   □
-------
3 5 1 2
```

14.
```
  5 □ 1
× 5
-------
2 9 0 5
```

15.
```
  3 □ 9
× 2
-----
7 9 8
```

16.
```
  6 2 4
×   □
-------
4 9 9 2
```

17.
```
  4 3 □
× 8
-------
3 5 0 4
```

18.
```
  5 9 7
×   □
-------
1 1 9 4
```

What's Missing?

Devilish Dilbert is blamed for the disappearing dividends.
Help him return them by writing the missing dividends.

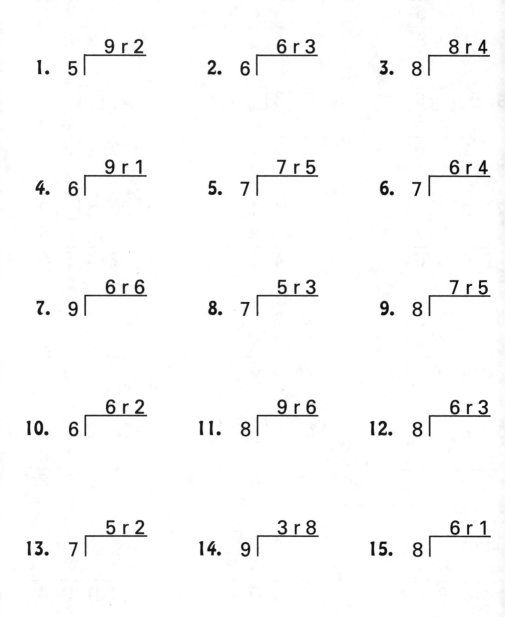

1. 5 ⟌ 9 r 2

2. 6 ⟌ 6 r 3

3. 8 ⟌ 8 r 4

4. 6 ⟌ 9 r 1

5. 7 ⟌ 7 r 5

6. 7 ⟌ 6 r 4

7. 9 ⟌ 6 r 6

8. 7 ⟌ 5 r 3

9. 8 ⟌ 7 r 5

10. 6 ⟌ 6 r 2

11. 8 ⟌ 9 r 6

12. 8 ⟌ 6 r 3

13. 7 ⟌ 5 r 2

14. 9 ⟌ 3 r 8

15. 8 ⟌ 6 r 1

Supply the missing divisors, quotients, factors, or products. Then write the letters to the corresponding answers on the lines below to solve the riddle.

1. 54 ÷ 9 = _____ **L**

2. 56 = 8 x _____ **L**

3. 9 = 27 ÷ _____ **R**

4. 45 ÷ _____ = 9 **U**

5. 32 ÷ _____ = 8 **!**

6. _____ = 4 x 3 **E**

7. 63 ÷ 7 = _____ **P**

8. 6 x 7 = _____ **T**

9. 36 ÷ _____ = 18 **M**

10. 48 = 6 x _____ **I**

11. 64 = 8 x _____ **I**

12. 9 x _____ = 99 **S**

What kind of pliers do you use in math?

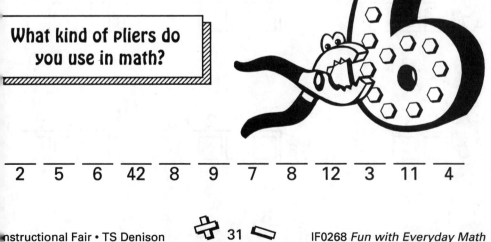

2	5	6	42	8	9	7	8	12	3	11	4

Divide and Conquer

Use the following steps to find the missing dividend.

1. Multiply the quotient by the divisor.

2. Add the remainder to this product.

3. Write the answer in the dividend boxes.

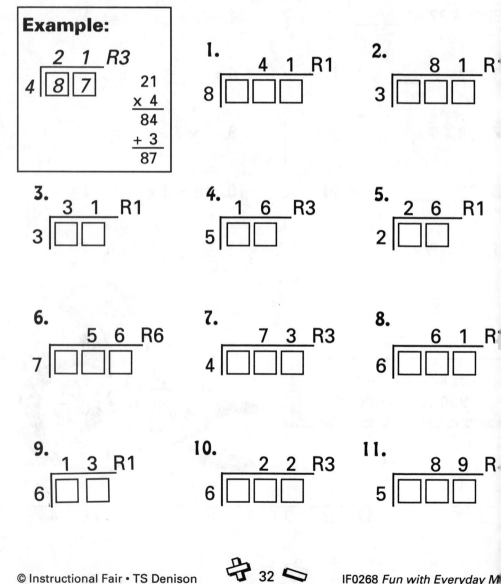

Example:

```
      2  1  R3
   _____
4 | 8 | 7 |        21
                 × 4
                ____
                  84
                 + 3
                ____
                  87
```

1.
```
      4  1  R1
   _____
8 | □ □ □
```

2.
```
      8  1  R
   _____
3 | □ □ □
```

3.
```
     3  1  R1
  _____
3 | □ □
```

4.
```
     1  6  R3
  _____
5 | □ □
```

5.
```
     2  6  R1
  _____
2 | □ □
```

6.
```
      5  6  R6
  _____
7 | □ □ □
```

7.
```
      7  3  R3
  _____
4 | □ □ □
```

8.
```
      6  1  R
  _____
6 | □ □ □
```

9.
```
     1  3  R1
  _____
6 | □ □
```

10.
```
      2  2  R3
  _____
6 | □ □ □
```

11.
```
      8  9  R
  _____
5 | □ □ □
```

olve these division problems. Write the letters to the
rresponding answers below to solve the riddle.

M
1. $55\overline{)715}$

L
2. $27\overline{)895}$

H
3. $68\overline{)826}$

P
4. $46\overline{)966}$

B
5. $42\overline{)983}$

A
6. $34\overline{)816}$

A
7. $36\overline{)900}$

C
8. $52\overline{)572}$

O
9. $16\overline{)499}$

What do you get if your sheep
studies karate?

25	33	24	13	23	11	12	31	21
	r4			r 17		r 10	r 3	

Missing Operations

Place the correct mathematical sign (+, −, x, ÷) in each box
to complete the number sentence.

56 ☐ 8 = 7   42 ☐ 6 = 7   17 ☐ 9 = 8

8 ☐ 6 = 14   9 ☐ 9 = 18   32 ☐ 8 = 4

32 ☐ 27 = 5   54 ☐ 12 = 66   11 ☐ 9 = 2

9 ☐ 3 = 27   15 ☐ 7 = 8   64 ☐ 8 = 8

16 ☐ 4 = 4   9 ☐ 8 = 72   45 ☐ 9 = 5

18 ☐ 9 = 9   12 ☐ 4 = 3   6 ☐ 8 = 4

8 ☐ 5 = 13   7 ☐ 7 = 49   21 ☐ 7 = 3

6 ☐ 7 = 42   36 ☐ 6 = 30   42 ☐ 16 =

11 ☐ 5 = 6   27 ☐ 3 = 9   35 ☐ 5 = 4

6 ☐ 4 = 24   8 ☐ 8 = 16   16 ☐ 2 = 8

ork from the inside or the outside of the circle to fill
the missing quotients. Then unscramble the letters
circling each wheel to spell the answer to the riddle.

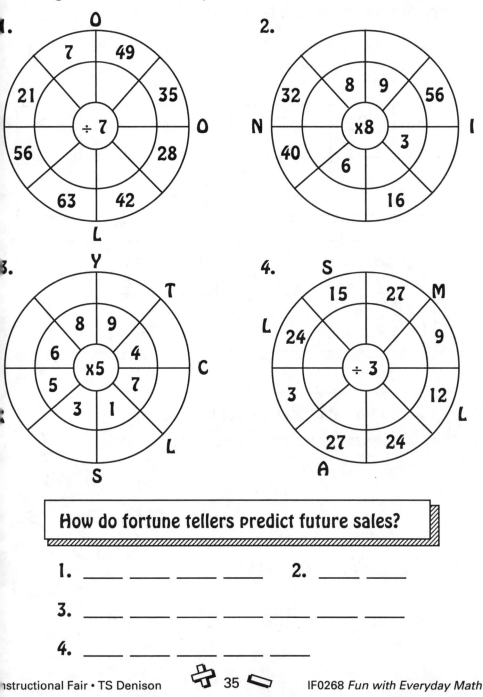

1. O — 7 49 21 35 ÷7 O 56 28 63 42 L

2. 8 9 32 56 N x8 3 40 6 I 16

3. Y T 8 9 6 4 x5 C 5 7 3 1 L S

4. S 15 27 M L 24 9 3 ÷3 12 L 27 24 A

How do fortune tellers predict future sales?

1. ___ ___ ___ ___   2. ___ ___

3. ___ ___ ___ ___ ___ ___ ___ ___

4. ___ ___ ___ ___

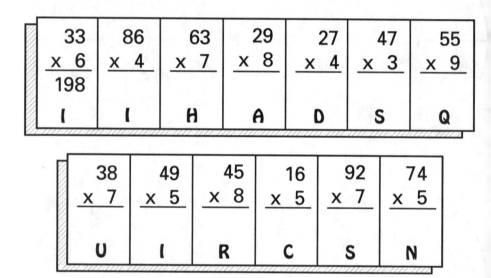

Time for Riddles

Find the products. Then match the letters with the corresponding answers below to answer the riddle.

33 x 6 = 198	86 x 4	63 x 7	29 x 8	27 x 4	47 x 3	55 x 9
I	I	H	A	D	S	Q

38 x 7	49 x 5	45 x 8	16 x 5	92 x 7	74 x 5
U	I	R	C	S	N

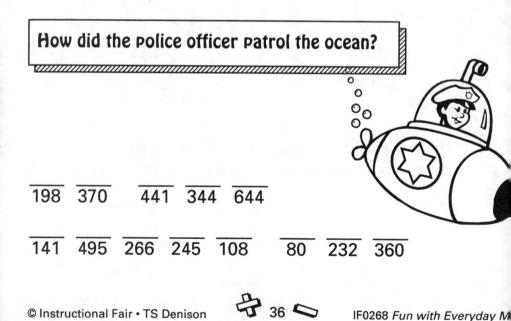

How did the police officer patrol the ocean?

‾‾‾ ‾‾‾   ‾‾‾ ‾‾‾ ‾‾‾
198 370   441 344 644

‾‾‾ ‾‾‾ ‾‾‾ ‾‾‾ ‾‾‾   ‾‾‾ ‾‾‾ ‾‾‾
141 495 266 245 108   80 232 360

IF0268 Fun with Everyday M

Answer Key

Fun With Everyday Math

Grade 4

---

lute to Sequencing

dy each sequence. Draw the next four logical pictures
e sequence.

uctional Fair • TS Denison   4   IF0268 Fun with Everyday Math

---

Look at the numbers in each flag. Read the rule, then
write the next four numbers of the pattern.

Bonus—Extend the number patterns in each flag as far as
you wish.

© Instructional Fair • TS Denison   5   IF0268 Fun with Everyday Math

---

Round and Round

Round each number to the nearest . . .

ten.   57 $\underline{60}$ 85 $\underline{90}$ 77 $\underline{80}$ 97 $\underline{100}$
        42 $\underline{40}$ 16 $\underline{20}$ 33 $\underline{30}$ 45 $\underline{50}$

hundred.   116 $\underline{100}$ 784 $\underline{800}$ 345 $\underline{300}$
            571 $\underline{600}$ 901 $\underline{900}$ 650 $\underline{700}$
            350 $\underline{400}$ 446 $\underline{400}$ 891 $\underline{900}$

thousand.   3,783 $\underline{4,000}$ 2,520 $\underline{3,000}$
             4,015 $\underline{4,000}$ 7,500 $\underline{8,000}$
             2,067 $\underline{2,000}$ 4,474 $\underline{4,000}$
             1,814 $\underline{2,000}$ 6,642 $\underline{7,000}$
             5,789 $\underline{6,000}$ 8,417 $\underline{8,000}$

Round the approximate distances between these cities to
the nearest thousand.

	Miles	Nearest Thousand
Albany, NY to San Francisco, CA	3,146	3,000
Albuquerque, NM to Boston, MA	2,220	2,000
Hartford, CT to St. Louis, MO	1,079	1,000

© Instructional Fair • TS Denison   6   IF0268 Fun with Everyday Math

---

Watiz Yer Zip, the mathematical postman, uses city zip
es to practice his rounding skills. Help him complete
chart.

Cities	Zip Codes	Round to Hundreds	Round to Thousands
stin, TX	78711	78,700	79,000
lem, OR	97310	97,300	97,000
nsing, MI	48909	48,900	49,000
s Moines, IA	50309	50,300	50,000
neau, AK	99811	99,800	100,000
cramento, CA	95814	95,800	96,000
lumbus, OH	43266	43,300	43,000
nta Fe, NM	87503	87,500	88,000
icago, IL	60601	60,600	61,000
anta, GA	30301	30,300	30,000
chmond, VA	23219	23,200	23,000
Paul, MN	55101	55,100	55,000
nolulu, HI	96815	96,800	97,000
lahassee, FL	32301	32,300	32,000

uctional Fair • TS Denison   7   IF0268 Fun with Everyday Math

---

Comparatively Speaking

Write the answer to each problem on the line. Then write
<, >, or = in each box to compare the numbers.

16 ÷ 4 $\boxed{=}$ 32 ÷ 8   4 × 5 $\boxed{>}$ 9 ÷ 3
$\underline{4}$ $\underline{4}$ $\underline{20}$ $\underline{3}$

54 ÷ 6 $\boxed{>}$ 49 ÷ 7   6 × 8 $\boxed{<}$ 7 × 7
$\underline{9}$ $\underline{7}$ $\underline{48}$ $\underline{49}$

42 ÷ 6 $\boxed{=}$ 49 ÷ 7   7 × 8 $\boxed{<}$ 6 × 9
$\underline{7}$ $\underline{7}$ $\underline{56}$ $\underline{54}$

4 × 7 $\boxed{>}$ 8 × 3   48 ÷ 8 $\boxed{>}$ 15 ÷ 5
$\underline{28}$ $\underline{24}$ $\underline{6}$ $\underline{3}$

4 × 9 $\boxed{=}$ 6 × 6   4 × 2 $\boxed{<}$ 72 ÷ 8
$\underline{36}$ $\underline{36}$ $\underline{8}$ $\underline{9}$

32 ÷ 8 $\boxed{=}$ 28 ÷ 7   45 ÷ 9 $\boxed{>}$ 20 ÷ 5
$\underline{4}$ $\underline{4}$ $\underline{5}$ $\underline{4}$

© Instructional Fair • TS Denison   8   IF0268 Fun with Everyday Math

---

Compare these numbers by writing <, >, or = in each
circle. Then find the author of the book, *Tales of a Fourth
Grade Nothing.*

Y 463,772 $>$ 436,272   A 212,121 $<$ 212,221
U 990,563 $>$ 909,418   J 583,754 $>$ 583,574
S 381,915 $<$ 381,951   Z 101,001 $<$ 101,101
L 671,048 $>$ 671,048   K 489,999 $=$ 489,999
T 632,791 $<$ 632,891   M 846,197 $>$ 846,179
D 51,010 $>$ 51,001   F 489,689 $<$ 489,697
E 707,414 $>$ 707,144   D 862,471 $<$ 862,714
B 911,300 $>$ 911,030   U 742,958 $>$ 742,856

YULDEBJMU

Record the letters of the problems with > as the answer.
Then unscramble them to discover the author's name.

JUDY BLUME

© Instructional Fair • TS Denison   9   IF0268 Fun with Everyday Math

---

Race Station Estimation

The famous race car driver, S. Tim Ate, needs your help to estimate the sums or differences for these problems. Read each problem. Round the numbers and write your estimate on the line. Remember to label your answers.

1. The top three NASCAR races had 43, 28, and 24 cars entered. About how many entered? **90 cars**

2. Sam Speedy finished the race in 58 minutes. Barney Blowout finished in 84 minutes. About how many minutes faster did Sam finish? **20 minutes**

3. The Tire Troopers changed 37 tires in May, 65 in June, and 73 in July. About how many tires did they change in all? **180 tires**

4. During August, Pete Piston entered races with distances of 316, 450, and 287 miles. About how many miles did Pete race in August? **1100 miles**

5. This summer 89 cars were involved in crashes. Last year, only 65 were involved in crashes. About how many more crashed this summer? **20 cars**

6. In the last 5 years, the Indy 500 has had 33 cars race each year. About how many cars raced during this 5-year period? **150 cars**

The kids who live near BJ's Fun Park were practicing for the fall go-cart races. Round the numbers and estimate the total number of laps each child practiced during the summer months. Then calculate the actual amount of total laps and average per month to the nearest lap.

Driver	Practice Laps			Estimate of Total Laps	Actual Total Laps	Average Laps Per Month
	June	July	Aug.			
Shelly	53	62	68	180	183	61
Andy	47	56	58	170	161	54
Sydney	57	65	68	200	190	63
Tyesha	57	65	68	200	190	63
Toby	43	41	46	130	130	43
Hannah	50	55	53	160	158	53
Mika	46	52	48	150	146	49
José	52	53	49	150	154	51
Myra	48	37	51	140	136	45
Kurt	61	58	53	170	172	57
Morgan	68	74	69	210	211	70
Cassandra	48	45	49	150	142	47
Jordan	54	46	50	150	150	50

What's the Difference?

Find the difference for each problem. Then write the letters to the corresponding answers on the lines below to solve the riddle.

1. $600.04 − 1.76 = $**598.28** A

2. $700.40 − 27.15 = $**673.25** S

3. $200 − 66 = $**133.**

4. $500.00 − 320.60 = $**179.40** S

5. $101.10 − 64.92 = $**36.18** I

6. $30 − 21 = $**8**

7. $805.05 − 371.59 = $**433.46** I

8. $500.50 − 193.76 = $**306.74** S

9. $404 − 272 = $**131.**

What kind of fish is a bargain?

A **S A I L F I S**
   $673.25 $598.28 $433.46 $131.74 $86.84 $36.18 $179.40

Solve each problem. Shade answers that appear on the Bingo card. Then draw a line through the winning row.

1. 7,136 − 2,298 = **4,838**
2. 8,430 − 2,554 = **5,876**
3. 5,032 − 2,774 = **2,258**
4. 3,002 − 1,596 = **1,406**
5. 2,145 − 1,989 = **156**
6. 7,818 − 5,446 = **2,372**
7. 9,014 − 2,565 = **6,449**
8. 4,141 − 2,067 = **2,074**
9. 1,042 − 209 = **833**
10. 8,612 − 4,754 = **3,858**
11. 9,155 − 3,083 = **6,072**
12. 4,313 − 2,246 = **2,067**

B I N G O

B	I	N	G	O
867	1,049	232	198	4,838
1,776	1,406	1,492	383	6,903
4,151	2,248	3,858	201	5,758
2,372	5,858	1,440	1,150	
1,997	2,074	5,771	700	6,449

Missing Addends

The Number Muncher has been eliminating addends from these problems! Write the missing numbers in each square.

1. 5 3 5 **4** + 2 **6** 7 8 = 8,0 3 2
2. 3 **0** 7 6 + 8 1 7 **5** = 11,9 5 1
3. **4** 3 **8** 2 + 3 2 6 **8** = 7,6 5 0
4. 2 5 **7** 1 1 5 + **5** 7 8 = 9 5 0
5. 6 0 4 **7** 5 **6** + 6 7 **8** = 2,0 3 8
6. **6** 3 **5** 3 4 7 + 9 **3** 4 = 2,1 1 6
7. 4 6 7 8 2 **2** 3 8 + 1 5 **1** 1 **9** = 8,4 3 5
8. 2 1 **7** 6 **3** 3 4 9 + 5 **3** 2 5 = 11,1 5 0
9. 1 **7** 4 1 3 2 **1** **2** + 2 **3** 7 8 = 7,9 4 5
10. 5 **4** 6 3 **3** 4 9 2 + 7 7 7 **0** = 22,2 3 4
11. **4** 7 3 4 2 **7** 6 8 + 5 6 6 **8** = 18,1 7 0
12. 7 5 **6** **5** 3 9 9 5 + 3 **8** 7 4 = 15,2 3 7

Show off your addition skills by adding the numbers [in] these problems. Remember to place commas in the answers. Then write the letters to the corresponding answers on the lines below to solve the riddle.

1. 11,565 + 89,248 = **100,813** U
2. 32,176 + 74,148 = **106,324** N
3. 85,4.. + .. = **103,9..**
4. 7,427 + 8,491 + 5,565 = **21,483** G
5. 9,462 + 8,153 + 3,976 = **21,591** B
6. 3,6.. 7,2.. + 9,8.. = **20,7..**
7. 4,877 + 3,251 + 9,464 + 3,849 = **21,441** U
8. 3,507 + 9,884 + 6,442 + 1,746 = **21,579** S
9. 7,8.. 1,9.. 8,3.. + 5,3.. = **23,3..**

What do you get if you cross an insect and a rabbit?

B U G S   B U N N
21,591 100,813 21,483 21,579   20,731 21,441 103,995 106,324

Get It Right

Take a bite out of subtraction. Donald Difference did that! Now it's up to you to put the "bites" back by writing the missing digits for these subtraction problems.

1. 8 5 **6** − 5 **7** 8 = 2 7 9
2. **4** 9 5 − 6 3 **6** = 1 5 9
3. 6 **8** 6 − 2 1 **8** = 4 6 8
4. 5 **7** 2 3 − 2 0 1 **5** = 3,3 0 8
5. **6** 0 6 0 − 3 3 **5** 9 = 4,6 8 1
6. **6** 2 1 **4** − 5 6 9 8 = 3,5 1 6
7. 8 **6** 5 3 0 − 7 2 4 **4** 1 = 1 4,0 8 9
8. 7 5 **6** 1 4 − 1 **8** 7 8 **6** = 5 7,4 2 8
9. 3 0 1 4 **9** − 6 6 **7** 0 5 = 2 3,4 4 7
10. **6** 3 1 9 2 − 2 6 **4** 3 2 = 6,7 6 0
11. 8 **8** 4 3 1 − **4** 9 5 5 4 = 3 **8** 8 7 7
12. **4** 8 3 3 3 − 1 6 **7** 4 **7** = 3 1,5 8 6

Pamela Perfect would like you to check her math problems so she can get a perfect score. Check problems using addition and circle any incorrect problems.

Example:
1,847 − 359 = 1,498 → 1,498 + 359 = 1,857

1. 976 − 392 = 584 → 584 + 392 = **976**

2. 1,892 − 566 = 1,326 → 1,326 + 566 = **1892**

3. 2,747 − 1,283 = 1,454 → 1,454 + 1,283 = **2737**

4. 7,494 − 5,688 = 1,806 → 1,806 + 5,688 = **7494**

5. 8,951 − 2,497 = 6,454 → 6,454 + 2,497 = **8951**

6. 3,466 − 575 = 2,891 → 575 + 2,891 = **3466**

7. 4,000 − 2,674 = 1,325 → 1,325 + 2,674 = **3999**

8. 7,216 − 4,588 = 2,628 → 2,628 + 4,588 = **7216**

9. 1,925 − 396 = 1,671 → 1,671 + 396 = **2067**

Don't Be "Coin"fused!

Help the clerk determine your change. The most effic[ient] way to count change is to start with the cost of the ite[m] and count to the amount of cash given. Draw the mo[ney] you would receive using the least amount of bills and coins. Use these symbol: $5 $1 ⓠ ⓓ Ⓝ

Cost of Item	Amount Given	Your change is . . .
$2.97	$5.00	ⓟ ⓟ ⓟ $1 $1
$5.68	$10.00	ⓟ ⓟ ⓓ ⓓ ⓝ $1 $1 $1 $1
$14.27	$15.00	ⓟ ⓟ ⓟ ⓓ ⓝ ⓠ ⓠ
$3.64	$5.00	ⓟ ⓓ ⓠ $1
$10.68	$20.00	ⓟ ⓟ ⓟ ⓓ ⓝ $1 $1 $1 $1 $1
$1.99	$5.00	ⓟ $1 $1 $1
$16.75	$20.00	ⓠ $1 $1 $1
$12.47	$15.00	ⓟ ⓟ ⓟ ⓓ ⓝ $1 $1

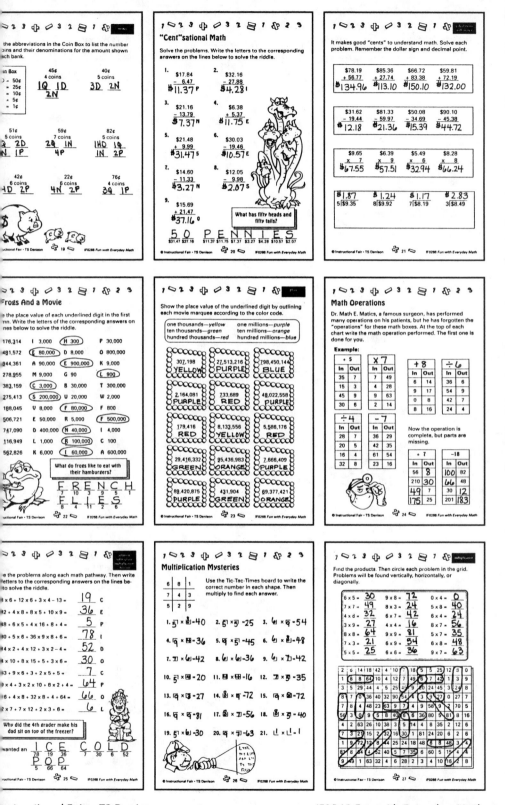

(Coin Box worksheet)

the abbreviations in the Coin Box to list the number
oins and their denominations for the amount shown
ach bank.

in Box	45¢ 4 coins	40¢ 5 coins
) = 50¢	1Q 1D	3D 2N
= 25¢	2N	
= 10¢		
= 5¢		
= 1¢		

51¢ 5 coins	59¢ 7 coins	82¢ 5 coins
2D	2Q 1N	1HD 1Q
1P	4P	1N 2P

42¢ 6 coins	22¢ 6 coins	76¢ 4 coins
1D 2P	4N 2P	3Q 1P

"Cent"sational Math

Solve the problems. Write the letters to the corresponding
answers on the lines below to solve the riddle.

1.
$17.84
− 6.47
$11.37 P

2.
$32.16
− 27.88
$4.28 I

3.
$21.16
− 13.79
$7.37 N

4.
$6.38
+ 5.37
$11.75 E

5.
$21.48
+ 9.99
$31.47 S

6.
$30.03
− 19.46
$10.57 E

7.
$14.60
− 11.33
$3.27 N

8.
$12.05
− 9.98
$2.07 S

9.
$15.69
+ 21.47
$37.16 O

What has fifty heads and
fifty tails?

5 0   P E N N I E S
$31.47 $37.16 $11.37 $11.75 $3.27 $4.28 $10.57 $2.07

It makes good "cents" to understand math. Solve each
problem. Remember the dollar sign and decimal point.

$78.19 + 56.77 = $134.96	$85.36 + 27.74 = $113.10	$66.72 + 83.38 = $150.10	$59.81 + 72.19 = $132.00
$31.62 − 19.44 = $12.18	$81.33 − 59.97 = $21.36	$50.08 − 34.69 = $15.39	$90.10 − 45.38 = $44.72
$9.65 x 7 = $67.55	$6.39 x 9 = $57.51	$5.49 x 6 = $32.94	$8.28 x 8 = $66.24
$1.87 5)$9.35	$1.24 8)$9.92	$1.17 7)$8.19	$2.83 3)$8.49

Frogs And a Movie

e the place value of each underlined digit in the first
nn. Write the letters of the corresponding answers on the
nes below to solve the riddle.

176,314	I 3,000	(H 300)	P 30,000
481,572	(E 80,000)	D 8,000	O 800,000
944,361	A 90,000	(E 900,000)	K 9,000
278,955	M 9,000	G 90	(L 900)
383,159	(C 3,000)	B 30,000	T 300,000
275,413	(S 200,000)	U 20,000	W 2,000
188,045	V 8,000	(F 80,000)	F 800
506,721	E 50,000	R 5,000	(F 500,000)
747,090	D 400,000	(N 40,000)	I 4,000
116,949	L 1,000	(R 100,000)	C 100
562,826	K 6,000	(I 60,000)	A 600,000

What do frogs like to eat with
their hamburgers?

F R E N C H
3 9 5 1

F L I E S
8 4 11 2 6

(Place value movie marquee)

Show the place value of the underlined digit by outlining
each movie marquee according to the color code.

one thousands—yellow   one millions—purple
ten thousands—green   ten millions—orange
hundred thousands—red hundred millions—blue

307,198 YELLOW   27,513,216 PURPLE   798,450,144 BLUE

2,164,081 PURPLE   733,689 RED   48,032,558 PURPLE

179,416 RED   8,133,556 YELLOW   5,586,176 RED

29,416,332 GREEN   95,436,983 ORANGE   7,666,409 PURPLE

89,420,875 PURPLE   431,904 GREEN   69,377,421 ORANGE

Math Operations

Dr. Math E. Matics, a famous surgeon, has performed
many operations on his patients, but he has forgotten the
"operations" for these math boxes. At the top of each
chart write the math operation performed. The first one is
done for you.

Example:

+ 5	
In	Out
35	7
15	3
45	9
30	6

X 7	
In	Out
7	49
4	28
9	63
2	14

+ 8	
In	Out
6	14
9	17
0	8
8	16

÷ 6	
In	Out
36	6
54	9
42	7
24	4

÷ 4	
In	Out
28	7
20	5
16	4
32	8

− 7	
In	Out
36	29
42	35
61	54
23	16

Now the operation is
complete, but parts are
missing.

+ 7	
In	Out
56	8
210	30
49	7
175	25

−18	
In	Out
100	82
66	48
30	12
201	183

(Math pathways worksheet)

e the problems along each math pathway. Then write
letters to the corresponding answers on the lines be-
to solve the riddle.

8 x 6 + 12 x 6 + 3 x 4 − 13 = 19 C
2 + 4 x 8 + 8 x 5 + 10 x 9 = 36 E
48 + 6 x 5 + 4 x 16 + 8 + 4 = 5 P
0 + 5 x 6 + 36 x 9 x 8 + 6 = 78 I
4 x 2 + 4 x 12 + 3 x 2 − 4 = 52 D
x 10 + 8 x 15 + 5 + 3 x 6 = 30 O
3 + 9 x 6 + 3 + 2 x 5 + 5 = 7 C
x 4 + 3 x 2 x 10 + 8 x 2 + 4 = 64 P
6 + 4 x 8 + 32 x 8 + 4 + 64 = 66 O
2 x 7 + 7 x 12 + 2 x 3 + 6 = 6 L

Why did the 4th grader make his
dad sit on top of the freezer?

vanted an   I C E   C O L D
78 19 36   7 30 6 52

P O P
50 66 64

Multiplication Mysteries

6	8	1
7	4	3
5	2	9

Use the Tic-Tac-Times board to write the
correct number in each shape. Then
multiply to find each answer.

1. 5 x 8 = 40   2. 5 x 5 = 25   3. 6 x 9 = 54
4. 9 x 4 = 36   5. 9 x 5 = 45   6. 6 x 8 = 48
7. 7 x 6 = 42   8. 6 x 6 = 36   9. 6 x 7 = 42
10. 5 x 4 = 20   11. 9 x 2 = 16   12. 7 x 5 = 35
13. 9 x 3 = 27   14. 8 x 9 = 72   15. 9 x 8 = 72
16. 9 x 9 = 81   17. 8 x 7 = 56   18. 8 x 5 = 40
19. 5 x 6 = 30   20. 9 x 7 = 63   21. 1 x 1 = 1

Find the products. Then circle each problem in the grid.
Problems will be found vertically, horizontally, or
diagonally.

6 x 5 = 30   9 x 8 = 72   0 x 4 = 0
7 x 7 = 49   8 x 3 = 24   5 x 8 = 40
4 x 8 = 32   6 x 7 = 42   8 x 4 = 24
3 x 9 = 27   4 x 4 = 16   8 x 7 = 56
8 x 8 = 64   9 x 9 = 81   5 x 7 = 35
7 x 3 = 21   9 x 6 = 54   6 x 8 = 48
5 x 5 = 25   6 x 6 = 36   9 x 7 = 63

Instructional Fair • TS Denison

Master Multiplication

Compute these multiplication problems. Write the letters to the corresponding answers below to solve the riddle.

U
1. 38 ×17 = 646

E
2. 66 ×28 = 1848

U
3. 29 ×58 = 1682

R
4. 39 ×16 = 624

B
5. 47 ×27 = 1269

R
6. 22 ×90 = 1980

M
7. 76 ×59 = 4484

H
8. 63 ×74 = 4662

G
9. 26 ×98 = 2548

What do you get when you cross a bee and chopped meat?

H U M B U R G E R
4,662 1,682 4,484 1,269 646 624 2,548 1,848 1,980

© Instructional Fair • TS Denison   28   IF0268 Fun with Everyday Math

---

Write the missing factors for these problems.

1. 6 [8] × 6 = 408
2. [3] 4 × 5 = 170
3. 2 [6] × 8 = 208
4. [5] 6 × 5 = 280
5. 3 [1] 4 × 8 = 2512
6. [7] 4 5 × 3 = 2235
7. 2 9 [8] × 7 = 2086
8. 1 1 [4] × 4 = 456
9. 4 [9] 9 × 5 = 2495
10. [8] 2 3 × 9 = 7407
11. 3 7 [7] × 4 = 1508
12. 2 0 [7] × 7 = 1449
13. 8 7 8 × [4] = 3512
14. 5 [8] 1 × 5 = 2905
15. 3 [9] 9 × 2 = 798
16. 6 2 4 × [8] = 4992
17. 4 3 [8] × 8 = 3504
18. 5 9 7 × [2] = 1194

© Instructional Fair • TS Denison   29   IF0268 Fun with Everyday Math

---

What's Missing?

Devilish Dilbert is blamed for the disappearing divide. Help him return them by writing the missing dividend.

1. 5)47 9 r 2
2. 6)39 6 r 3
3. 8)68 8 r
4. 6)55 9 r 1
5. 7)54 7 r 5
6. 7)4(6 r
7. 9)60 6 r 6
8. 7)38 5 r 3
9. 8)61 7 r
10. 6)38 6 r 2
11. 8)78 9 r 6
12. 8)51 6 r
13. 7)37 5 r 2
14. 9)35 3 r 8
15. 8)4(6 r

© Instructional Fair • TS Denison   30   IF0268 Fun with Everyday Math

---

Supply the missing divisors, quotients, factors, or products. Then write the letters to the corresponding answers on the lines below to solve the riddle.

1. 54 ÷ 9 = 6 L
2. 56 = 8 × 7 L
3. 9 = 27 ÷ 3 R
4. 45 ÷ 5 = 9 U
5. 32 ÷ 4 = 8 I
6. 12 = 4 × 3 E
7. 63 ÷ 7 = 9 P
8. 6 × 7 = 42 T
9. 36 ÷ 2 = 18 M
10. 48 = 6 × 8 I
11. 64 = 8 × 8 I
12. 9 × 11 = 99 S

What kind of pliers do you use in math?

M U L T I P L I E R S !
2   5   6   42   8   9   7   8   12   3   11   4

© Instructional Fair • TS Denison   31   IF0268 Fun with Everyday Math

---

Divide and Conquer

Use the following steps to find the missing dividend.
1. Multiply the quotient by the divisor.
2. Add the remainder to this product.
3. Write the answer in the dividend boxes.

Example:
```
 2 1 R3
8 )87
   8
   ----
   21
   84
  + 3
  ----
   87
```

1. 8)32(4 1 R1
2. 3)24(8 1 R1
3. 3)94 3 1 R1
4. 5)83 1 6 R1
5. 2)53 2 6 R1
6. 7)34(5 6 R6
7. 4)29(7 3 R3
8. 6)36(6 1 R2
9. 6)79 1 3 R1
10. 6)135 2 2 R3
11. 5)449 8 9 R4

© Instructional Fair • TS Denison   32   IF0268 Fun with Everyday Math

---

Solve these division problems. Write the letters to the corresponding answers below to solve the riddle.

M
1. 55)715 13

L
2. 27)895 33 r.4

H
3. 68)826 12 r.10

P
4. 46)966 21

B
5. 42)983 23 r.17

A
6. 34)816 24

A
7. 36)900 25

C
8. 52)572 11

O
9. 16)499 31 r.3

What do you get if your sheep studies karate?

A L A M B C H O P
25 33 24 13 23 11 12 31 21
    r4   r 17   r 10 r 3

© Instructional Fair • TS Denison   33   IF0268 Fun with Everyday Math

---

What's Missing?

Place the correct mathematical sign (+, −, ×, ÷) in each box to complete the number sentence.

56 ÷ 8 = 7
8 + 6 = 14
32 ÷ 27 = 5
9 × 3 = 27
16 ÷ 4 = 4
18 − 9 = 9
8 + 5 = 13
6 × 7 = 42
11 − 5 = 6
6 × 4 = 24

42 ÷ 6 = 7
9 + 9 = 18
54 + 12 = 66
15 − 7 = 8
9 × 8 = 72
12 ÷ 4 = 3
7 × 7 = 49
36 − 6 = 30
27 + 3 = 9
8 + 8 = 16

17 − 9 = 8
32 ÷ 8 = 4
11 − 9 = 2
64 ÷ 8 = 8
45 + 9 = 5
6 × 8 = 48
21 ÷ 7 = 3
42 − 16 = 26
35 + 5 = 40
16 ÷ 2 = 8

© Instructional Fair • TS Denison   34   IF0268 Fun with Everyday Math

---

Work from the inside or the outside of the circle to fill in the missing factors. Then unscramble the letters encircling each wheel to spell the answer to the riddle.

How do fortune tellers predict future sales?

1. L O O K   2. I N
3. C R Y S T A L
4. B A L L S

© Instructional Fair • TS Denison   35   IF0268 Fun with Everyday Math

---

Time for Riddles

Find the products. Then match the letters with the corresponding answers below to answer the riddle.

| 33 ×6 =198 | 86 ×4 =344 | 63 ×7 =441 | 29 ×8 =232 | 27 ×4 =108 | 47 ×3 =141 | 55 ×9 =495 |
| I | H | A | D | S | O | |

| 38 ×7 =266 | 49 ×5 =245 | 45 ×8 =360 | 16 ×5 =80 | 92 ×7 =644 | 74 ×5 =370 |
| U | I | R | C | S | H |

How did the police officer patrol the ocean?

I N   H I S
198 370   441 344 644

S Q U I D   C A R
141 495 266 245 108   80 232 360

© Instructional Fair • TS Denison   36   IF0268 Fun with Everyday Math

---

© Instructional Fair • TS Denison   IF0268 Fun with Everyday M

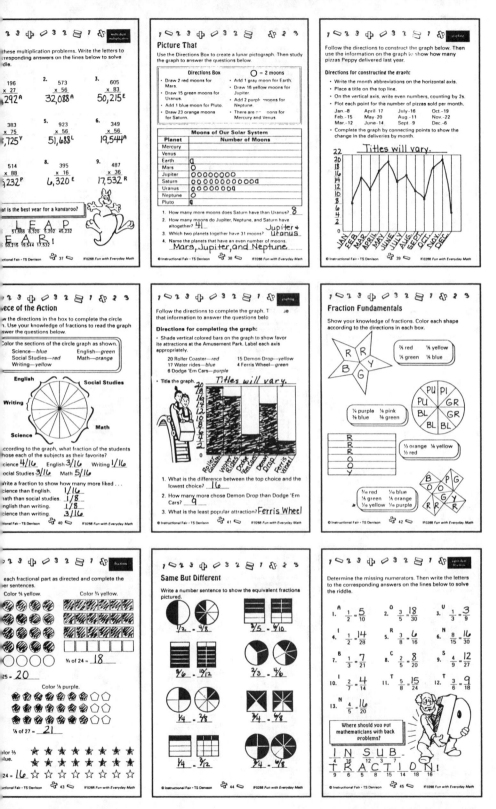

multi-digit multiplication

these multiplication problems. Write the letters to responding answers on the lines below to solve dle.

196 × 27 = ,292 A	2. 573 × 56 = 32,088 A	3. 605 × 83 = 50,215 E
383 × 75 = ,725 Y	5. 923 × 56 = 51,688 L	6. 349 × 56 = 19,544 A
514 × 88 = ,232 P	8. 395 × 16 = 6,320 E	9. 487 × 36 = 17,532 R

at is the best year for a kangaroo?

L E A P — 51,688 6,320 5,292 45,232

E A R ! — 50,215 19,544 17,532

Picture That

Use the Directions Box to create a lunar pictograph. Then study the graph to answer the questions below.

Directions Box ○ = 2 moons

- Draw 2 red moons for Mars.
- Draw 15 green moons for Uranus.
- Add 1 blue moon for Pluto.
- Draw 23 orange moons for Saturn.
- Add 1 gray moon for Earth.
- Draw 16 yellow moons for Jupiter.
- Add 2 purple moons for Neptune.
- There are no moons for Mercury and Venus.

Moons of Our Solar System

Planet	Number of Moons
Mercury	
Venus	
Earth	◐
Mars	○
Jupiter	○○○○○○○○
Saturn	○○○○○○○○○○○◐
Uranus	○○○○○○○◐
Neptune	○
Pluto	◐

1. How many more moons does Saturn have than Uranus? 8
2. How many moons do Jupiter, Neptune, and Saturn have altogether? 41
3. Which two planets together have 31 moons? Jupiter + Uranus
4. Name the planets that have an even number of moons. Mars, Jupiter, and Neptune

graphing

Follow the directions to construct the graph below. Then use the information on the graph to show how many pizzas Peppy delivered last year.

Directions for constructing the graph:

- Write the month abbreviations on the horizontal axis.
- Place a title on the top line.
- On the vertical axis, write even numbers, counting by 2s.
- Plot each point for the number of pizzas sold per month.

Jan.-8	April-17	July-16	Oct.-19
Feb.-15	May-20	Aug.-11	Nov.-22
Mar.-12	June-14	Sept.-9	Dec.-6

- Complete the graph by connecting points to show the change in the deliveries by month.

Titles will vary.

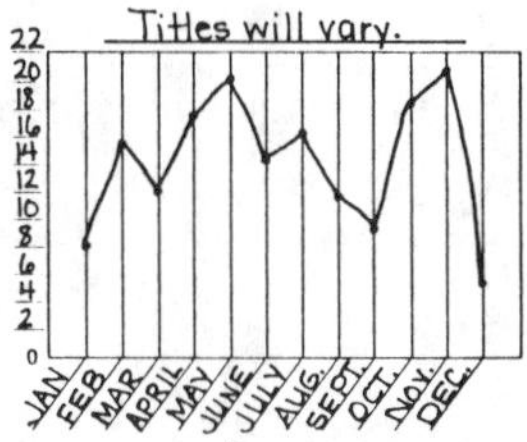
22
20
18
16
14
12
10
8
6
4
2
0
JAN FEB MAR APRIL MAY JUNE JULY AUG. SEPT. OCT. NOV. DEC.

ece of the Action

w the directions in the box to complete the circle n. Use your knowledge of fractions to read the graph swer the questions below.

Color the sections of the circle graph as shown.
Science—*blue* English—*green*
Social Studies—*red* Math—*orange*
Writing—*yellow*

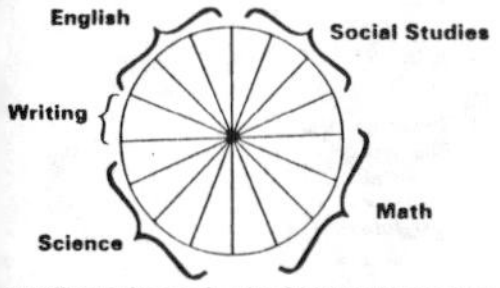
English
Social Studies
Writing
Math
Science

ccording to the graph, what fraction of the students hose each of the subjects as their favorite?

cience 4/16 English 3/16 Writing 1/16
ocial Studies 3/16 Math 5/16

Vrite a fraction to show how many more liked . . .
cience than English. 1/16
nath than social studies. 1/8
nglish than writing. 1/8
cience than writing. 3/16

graphing

Follow the directions to complete the graph. T ... se that information to answer the questions belo

Directions for completing the graph:

- Shade vertical colored bars on the graph to show favorite attractions at the Amusement Park. Label each axis appropriately.

20 Roller Coaster—*red* 15 Demon Drop—*yellow*
17 Water rides—*blue* 4 Ferris Wheel—*green*
6 Dodge 'Em Cars—*purple*

- Title the graph. Titles will vary.

20
18
16
14
12
10
8
6
4
2
0
Roller Coaster
Water Rides
Dodge 'Em Cars
Demon Drop
Ferris Wheel

1. What is the difference between the top choice and the lowest choice? 16
2. How many more chose Demon Drop than Dodge 'Em Cars? 9
3. What is the least popular attraction? Ferris Wheel

Fraction Fundamentals

Show your knowledge of fractions. Color each shape according to the directions in each box.

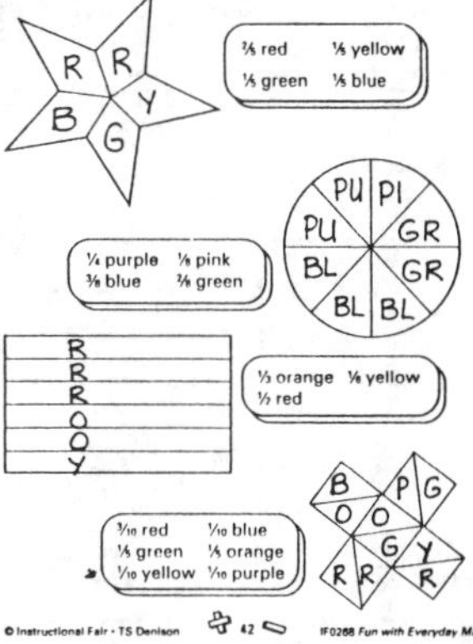
R R B G Y
⅖ red ⅕ yellow
⅕ green ⅕ blue
PU PI PU GR BL GR BL BL
¼ purple ⅛ pink
⅜ blue ²⁄₈ green
R R R O O Y
⅓ orange ⅙ yellow
½ red
B P G O O G Y R R R
³⁄₁₀ red ¹⁄₁₀ blue
⅕ green ⅕ orange
¹⁄₁₀ yellow ¹⁄₁₀ purple

fractions

each fractional part as directed and complete the er sentences.

Color ⅘ yellow. Color ¾ yellow.

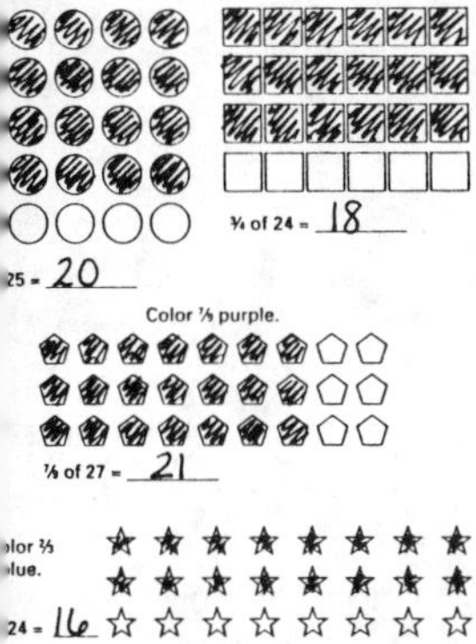

¾ of 24 = 18

25 = 20

Color ⁷⁄₉ purple.

⁷⁄₉ of 27 = 21

olor ⅔ lue.

24 = 16

Same But Different

Write a number sentence to show the equivalent fractions pictured.

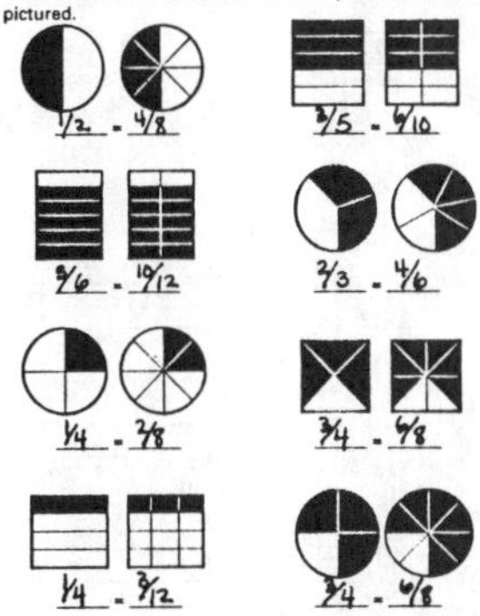

1/2 = 4/8 3/5 = 6/10
5/6 = 10/12 2/3 = 4/6
1/4 = 2/8 3/4 = 6/8
1/4 = 3/12 3/4 = 6/8

equivalent fractions

Determine the missing numerators. Then write the letters to the corresponding answers on the lines below to solve the riddle.

A 1. $\frac{1}{2} = \frac{5}{10}$	O 2. $\frac{3}{5} = \frac{18}{30}$	U 3. $\frac{1}{3} = \frac{3}{9}$
I 4. $\frac{1}{2} = \frac{14}{28}$	R 5. $\frac{3}{8} = \frac{6}{16}$	N 6. $\frac{8}{15} = \frac{16}{30}$
B 7. $\frac{1}{3} = \frac{7}{21}$	C 8. $\frac{2}{5} = \frac{8}{20}$	S 9. $\frac{4}{9} = \frac{12}{27}$
I 10. $\frac{2}{7} = \frac{4}{14}$	T 11. $\frac{5}{8} = \frac{15}{24}$	T 12. $\frac{3}{6} = \frac{9}{18}$
N 13. $\frac{4}{5} = \frac{16}{20}$		

Where should you put mathematicians with back problems?

I N S U B -
4 16 12 3 7

T R A C T I O N !
9 6 5 8 15 14 18 16

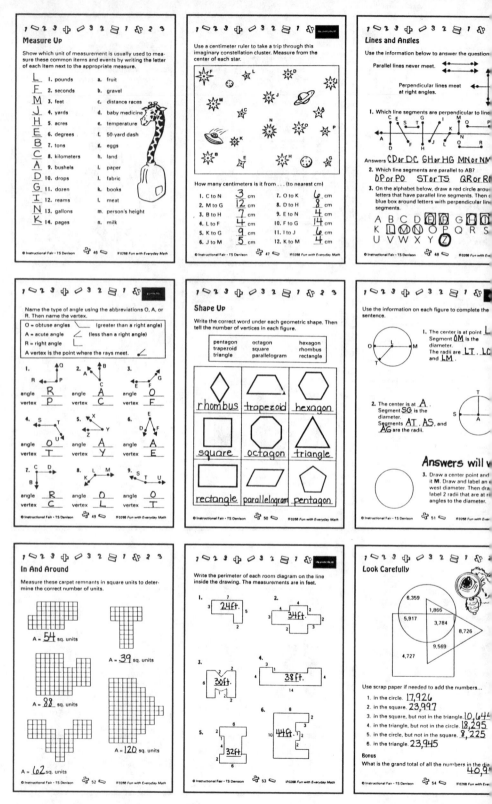

Measure Up

Show which unit of measurement is usually used to measure these common items and events by writing the letter of each item next to the appropriate measure.

L	1. pounds	a.	fruit
F	2. seconds	b.	gravel
M	3. feet	c.	distance races
J	4. yards	d.	baby medicine
H	5. acres	e.	temperature
E	6. degrees	f.	50-yard dash
B	7. tons	g.	eggs
C	8. kilometers	h.	land
A	9. bushels	i.	paper
D	10. drops	j.	fabric
G	11. dozen	k.	books
I	12. reams	l.	meat
N	13. gallons	m.	person's height
K	14. pages	n.	milk

Use a centimeter ruler to take a trip through this imaginary constellation cluster. Measure from the center of each star.

How many centimeters is it from . . . (to nearest cm)

1. C to N	3 cm		7. O to K	6 cm
2. M to G	12 cm		8. D to H	8 cm
3. B to H	7 cm		9. E to N	4 cm
4. L to F	4 cm		10. F to G	14 cm
5. K to G	9 cm		11. I to J	4 cm
6. J to M	5 cm		12. K to M	4 cm

Lines and Angles

Use the information below to answer the question

Parallel lines never meet.

Perpendicular lines meet at right angles.

1. Which line segments are perpendicular to line

Answers CD or DC GH or HG MN or NM

2. Which line segments are parallel to AB?

DP or PO ST or TS QR or R

3. On the alphabet below, draw a red circle arou letters that have parallel line segments. Then c blue box around letters with perpendicular line segments.

A B C D E F G H
K L M N O P Q R S
U V W X Y Z

Name the type of angle using the abbreviations O, A, or R. Then name the vertex.

O = obtuse angles (greater than a right angle)
A = acute angle (less than a right angle)
R = right angle
A vertex is the point where the rays meet.

1. angle R vertex P	2. angle A vertex C	3. angle O vertex F
4. angle O vertex T	5. angle A vertex Y	6. angle A vertex E
7. angle R vertex C	8. angle O vertex L	9. angle O vertex T

Shape Up

Write the correct word under each geometric shape. Then tell the number of vertices in each figure.

pentagon	octagon	hexagon
trapezoid	square	rhombus
triangle	parallelogram	rectangle

rhombus	trapezoid	hexagon
square	octagon	triangle
rectangle	parallelogram	pentagon

Use the information on each figure to complete the sentence.

1. The center is at point L
Segment OM is the diameter.
The radii are LT, LO and LM.

2. The center is at A.
Segment SG is the diameter.
Segments AT, AS, and AG are the radii.

Answers will v

3. Draw a center point and it M. Draw and label an e west diameter. Then dra label 2 radii that are at ri angles to the diameter.

In And Around

Measure these carpet remnants in square units to determine the correct number of units.

A = 54 sq. units

A = 39 sq. units

A = 88 sq. units

A = 120 sq. units

A = 62 sq. units

Write the perimeter of each room diagram on the line inside the drawing. The measurements are in feet.

1. 24ft.
2. 34ft.
3. 30ft.
4. 38ft.
5. 32ft.
6. 44ft.

Look Carefully

6,359		
	1,866	
5,917	3,784	
		8,726
9,569		
4,727		

Use scrap paper if needed to add the numbers...

1. in the circle. 17,926
2. in the square. 23,997
3. in the square, but not in the triangle. 10,641
4. in the triangle, but not in the circle. 18,295
5. in the circle, but not in the square. 8,225
6. in the triangle. 23,945

Bonus
What is the grand total of all the numbers in the dia
40,9

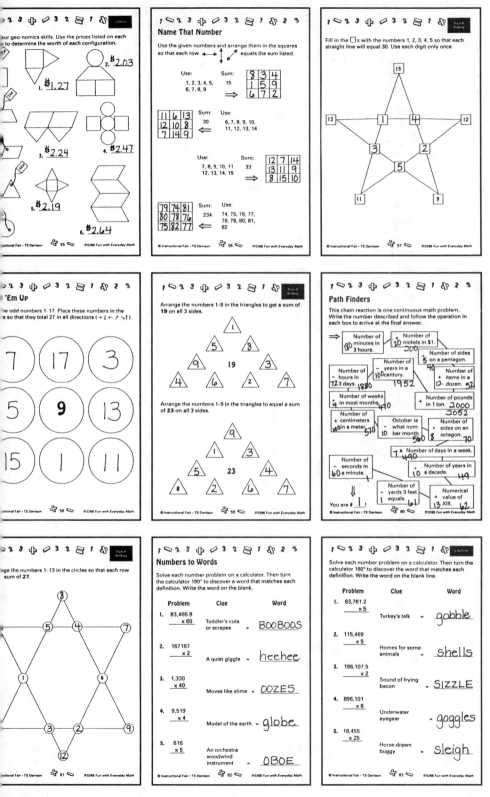

...ur geo-nomics skills. Use the prices listed on each ... to determine the worth of each configuration.

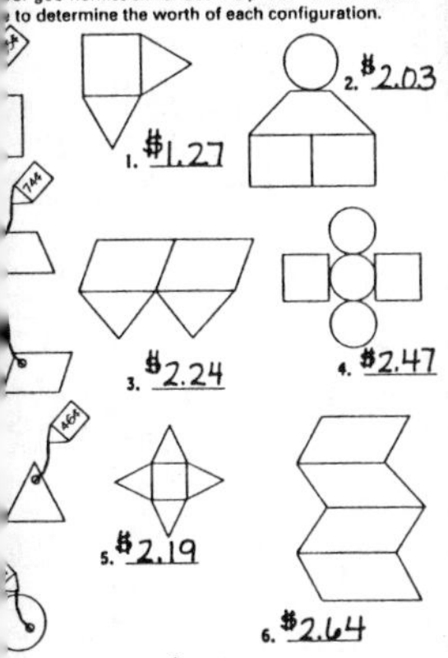

1. $1.27
2. $2.03
3. $2.24
4. $2.47
5. $2.19
6. $2.64

Name That Number

Use the given numbers and arrange them in the squares so that each row ↔ ↕ ⤢ equals the sum listed.

Use: 1, 2, 3, 4, 5, 6, 7, 8, 9 Sum: 15 ⇒

8	3	4
1	5	9
6	7	2

Sum: 30 Use: 6, 7, 8, 9, 10, 11, 12, 13, 14 ⇐

11	6	13
12	10	8
7	14	9

Use: 7, 8, 9, 10, 11 12, 13, 14, 15 Sum: 33 ⇒

12	7	14
13	11	9
8	15	10

Sum: 234 Use: 74, 75, 76, 77, 78, 79, 80, 81, 82 ⇐

79	74	81
80	78	76
75	82	77

Fill in the □s with the numbers 1, 2, 3, 4, 5 so that each straight line will equal 30. Use each digit only once.

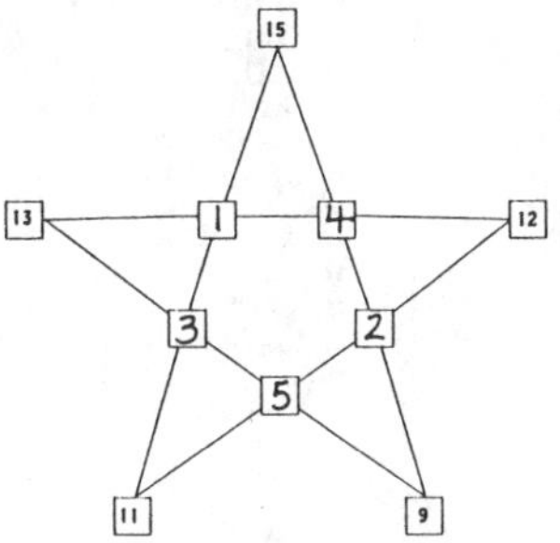

15
13
1
4
12
3
2
5
11
9

...'Em Up

...he odd numbers 1–17. Place these numbers in the ...s so that they total 27 in all directions (→ ↓ ← ↗ ↘ ↑).

7	17	3
5	**9**	13
15	1	11

Arrange the numbers 1–9 in the triangles to get a sum of **19** on all 3 sides.

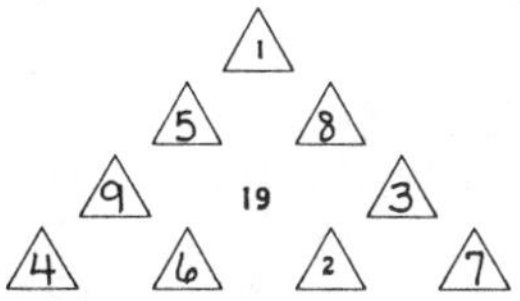

1
5
8
9
19
3
4
6
2
7

Arrange the numbers 1–9 in the triangles to equal a sum of **23** on all 3 sides.

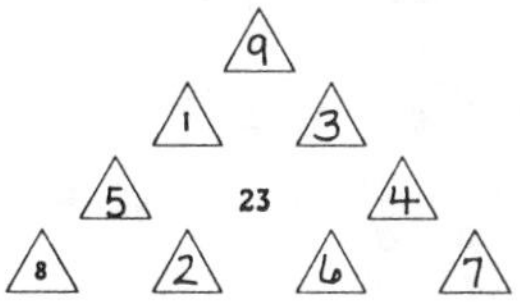

9
1
3
5
23
4
8
2
6
7

Path Finders

This chain reaction is one continuous math problem. Write the number described and follow the operation in each box to arrive at the final answer.

- ⇒ Number of minutes in 3 hours. 180
- + Number of nickels in $1. 20 — 200
- + Number of sides on a pentagon. 5 — 40
- + Number of items in a dozen. 12 — 52
- + Number of pounds in 1 ton. 2000 — 2052
- − Number of years in a century. 100 — 1952
- − Number of hours in 3 days. 72 — 1880
- + Number of weeks in most months. 4 — 470
- + Number of centimeters in a meter. 100 — 570
- − October is what number month. 10 — 560
- + Number of sides on an octagon. 8 — 70
- × Number of days in a week. 7 — 490
- + Number of years in a decade. 10 — 49
- + Numerical value of XIII. 13 — 62
- − Number of yards 3 feet equals. 1 — 61
- − Number of seconds in a minute. 60 — 1

⇓ You are # 1 !

...ge the numbers 1–13 in the circles so that each row ... sum of **27**.

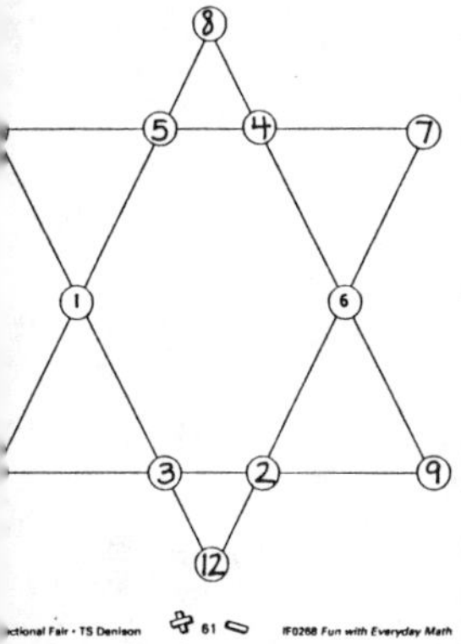

8
5
4
7
1
6
3
2
9
12

Numbers to Words

Solve each number problem on a calculator. Then turn the calculator 180° to discover a word that matches each definition. Write the word on the blank.

Problem	Clue	Word
1. 83,466.8 x 60	Toddler's cuts or scrapes =	BOOBOOS
2. 167167 x 2	A quiet giggle =	heehee
3. 1,330 x 40	Moves like slime =	OOZES
4. 9,519 x 4	Model of the earth =	globe
5. 616 x 5	An orchestra woodwind instrument =	OBOE

Solve each number problem on a calculator. Then turn the calculator 180° to discover the word that matches each definion. Write the word on the blank line.

Problem	Clue	Word
1. 63,761.2 x 5	Turkey's talk =	gobble
2. 115,469 x 5	Homes for some animals =	shells
3. 186,107.5 x 2	Sound of frying bacon =	SIZZLE
4. 896,101 x 6	Underwater eyegear =	goggles
5. 18,455 x 25	Horse-drawn buggy =	sleigh

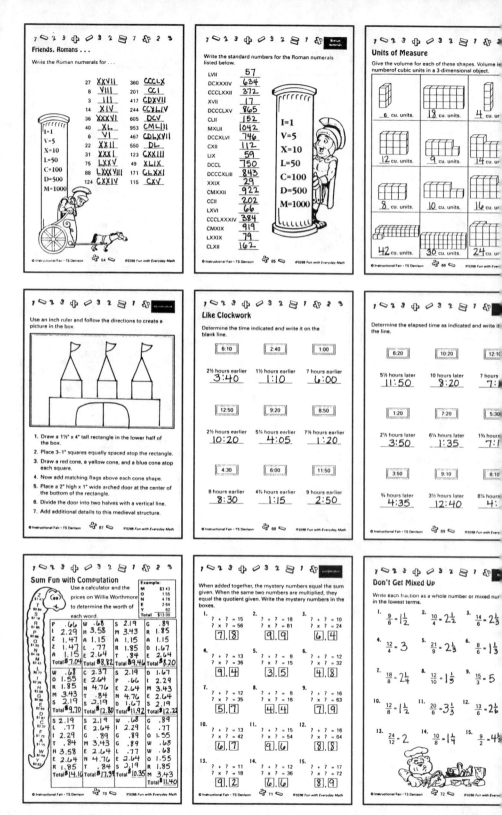

Friends, Romans . . .

Write the Roman numerals for . . .

27	XXVII	360	CCCLX
8	VIII	201	CCI
3	III	417	CDXVII
14	XIV	244	CCXLIV
36	XXXVI	605	DCV
40	XL	953	CMLIII
6	VI	467	CDLXVII
22	XXII	550	DL
31	XXXI	123	CXXIII
75	LXXV	49	XLIX
88	LXXXVIII	171	CLXXI
124	CXXIV	115	CXV

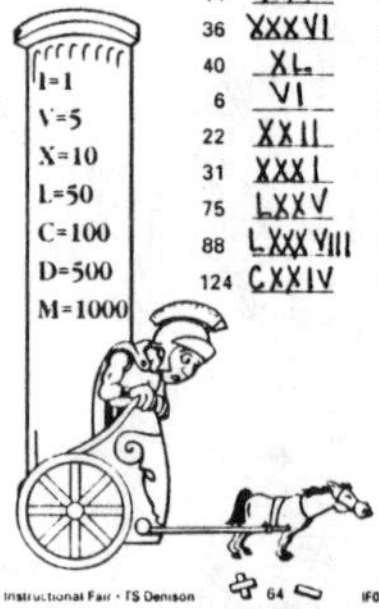

I=1
V=5
X=10
L=50
C=100
D=500
M=1000

Write the standard numbers for the Roman numerals listed below.

LVII	57
DCXXXIV	634
CCCLXXII	372
XVII	17
DCCCLXV	865
CLII	152
MXLII	1042
DCCXLVI	746
CXII	112
LIX	59
DCCL	750
DCCCXLIII	843
XXIX	29
CMXXII	922
CCII	202
LXVI	66
CCCLXXXIV	384
CMXIX	919
LXXIX	79
CLXII	162

I=1
V=5
X=10
L=50
C=100
D=500
M=1000

Units of Measure

Give the volume for each of these shapes. Volume is numberof cubic units in a 3-dimensional object.

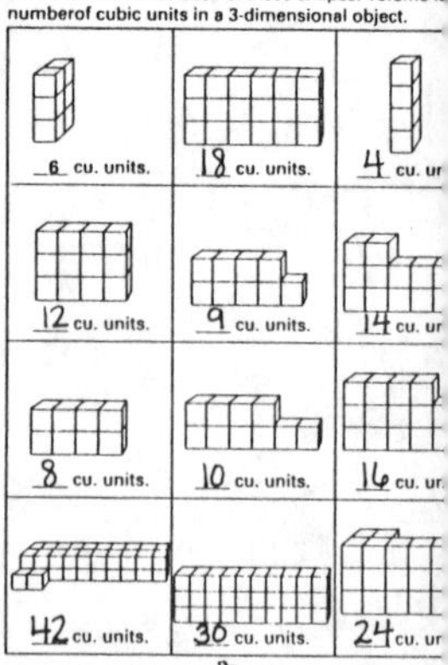

6 cu. units.	18 cu. units.	4 cu. un
12 cu. units.	9 cu. units.	14 cu. un
8 cu. units.	10 cu. units.	16 cu. un
42 cu. units.	30 cu. units.	24 cu. un

Use an inch ruler and follow the directions to create a picture in the box.

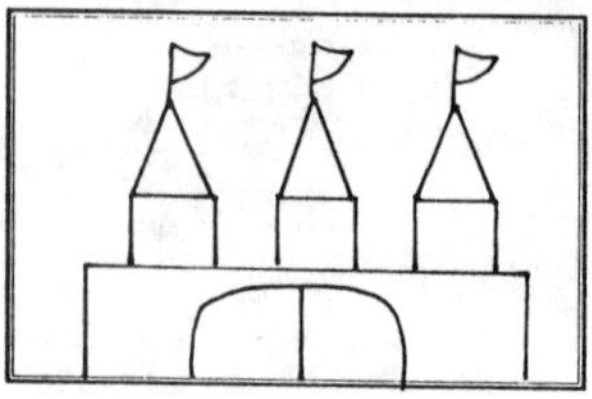

1. Draw a 1½" x 4" tall rectangle in the lower half of the box.
2. Place 3–1" squares equally spaced atop the rectangle.
3. Draw a red cone, a yellow cone, and a blue cone atop each square.
4. Now add matching flags above each cone shape.
5. Place a 2" high x 1" wide arched door at the center of the bottom of the rectangle.
6. Divide the door into two halves with a vertical line.
7. Add additional details to this medieval structure.

Like Clockwork

Determine the time indicated and write it on the blank line.

6:10	2:40	1:00
2½ hours earlier 3:40	1½ hours earlier 1:10	7 hours earlier 6:00
12:50	9:20	8:50
2½ hours earlier 10:20	5¼ hours earlier 4:05	7½ hours earlier 1:20
4:30	6:00	11:50
8 hours earlier 8:30	4¾ hours earlier 1:15	9 hours earlier 2:50

Determine the elapsed time as indicated and write it on the line.

6:20	10:20	12:10
5½ hours later 11:50	10 hours later 8:20	7 hours 7:
1:20	7:20	5:30
2½ hours later 3:50	6¼ hours later 1:35	1¾ hours 7:1
3:50	9:10	8:10
¾ hours later 4:35	3½ hours later 12:40	8¼ hours 4:

Sum Fun with Computation

Use a calculator and the prices on Willie Worthmore to determine the worth of each word.

Example:	
M	$3.43
O	1.55
N	4.76
E	2.64
Y	.62
Total	$13.00

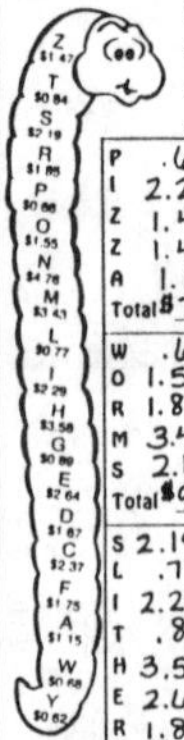

Z $1.47
T $0.84
S $2.19
R $1.85
P $0.66
O $1.55
N $4.76
M $3.43
L $0.77
I $2.29
H $3.58
G $0.89
E $2.64
D $1.67
C $2.37
F $1.75
A $1.15
W $0.68
Y $0.62

P .66 I 2.29 Z 1.47 Z 1.47 A 1.15 Total $7.04	W .68 H 3.58 A 1.15 L .77 E 2.64 Total $8.82	S 2.19 M 3.43 A 1.15 R 1.85 T .84 Total $9.46	G .89 R 1.85 A 1.15 D 1.67 E 2.64 Total $8.20
W .68 O 1.55 R 1.85 M 3.43 S 2.19 Total $9.70	C 2.37 E 2.64 N 4.76 T .84 S 2.19 Total $12.80	S 2.19 P .66 E 2.64 N 4.76 D 1.67 Total $11.92	D 1.67 I 2.29 M 3.43 E 2.64 S 2.19 Total $12.22
S 2.19 L .77 I 2.29 T .84 H 3.58 E 2.64 R 1.85 Total $14.16	S 2.19 E 2.64 G .89 M 3.43 E 2.64 N 4.76 T .84 Total $17.39	W .68 I 2.29 G .89 G .89 L .77 E 2.64 S 2.19 Total $10.35	G .89 L .77 O 1.55 W .68 W .68 O 1.55 R 1.85 M 3.43 Total $11.40

When added together, the mystery numbers equal the sum given. When the same two numbers are multiplied, they equal the quotient given. Write the mystery numbers in the boxes.

1. ? + ? = 15; ? x ? = 56 — 7, 8
2. ? + ? = 18; ? x ? = 81 — 9, 9
3. ? + ? = 10; ? x ? = 24 — 6, 4
4. ? + ? = 13; ? x ? = 36 — 9, 4
5. ? + ? = 8; ? x ? = 15 — 3, 5
6. ? + ? = 12; ? x ? = 32 — 4, 8
7. ? + ? = 12; ? x ? = 35 — 5, 7
8. ? + ? = 8; ? x ? = 16 — 4, 4
9. ? + ? = 16; ? x ? = 63 — 7, 9
10. ? + ? = 13; ? x ? = 42 — 6, 7
11. ? + ? = 15; ? x ? = 54 — 9, 6
12. ? + ? = 16; ? x ? = 64 — 8, 8
13. ? + ? = 11; ? x ? = 18 — 9, 2
14. ? + ? = 12; ? x ? = 36 — 6, 6
15. ? + ? = 17; ? x ? = 72 — 8, 9

Don't Get Mixed Up

Write each fraction as a whole number or mixed number in the lowest terms.

1. $\frac{9}{6} = 1\frac{1}{2}$
2. $\frac{10}{4} = 2\frac{1}{2}$
3. $\frac{14}{6} = 2\frac{1}{3}$
4. $\frac{12}{4} = 3$
5. $\frac{21}{9} = 2\frac{1}{3}$
6. $\frac{8}{6} = 1\frac{1}{3}$
7. $\frac{18}{8} = 2\frac{1}{4}$
8. $\frac{12}{10} = 1\frac{1}{5}$
9. $\frac{15}{3} = 5$
10. $\frac{12}{8} = 1\frac{1}{2}$
11. $\frac{20}{6} = 3\frac{1}{3}$
12. $\frac{13}{6} = 2\frac{1}{6}$
13. $\frac{24}{12} = 2$
14. $\frac{10}{8} = 1\frac{1}{4}$
15. $\frac{9}{2} = 4\frac{1}{2}$

lve these multiplication problems. Write the letters to
corresponding answers on the lines below to solve
riddle.

	2.		3.

196
x 27
A

2.
573
x 56
A

3.
605
x 83
E

383
x 75
Y

5.
923
x 56
L

6.
349
x 56
A

514
x 88
P

8.
395
x 16
E

9.
487
x 36
R

What is the best year for a kangaroo?

‾88   ‾51,688 ‾6,320 ‾5,292 ‾45,232

‾725 ‾50,215 ‾19,544 ‾17,532 **!**

1 ⬭ 2 3 ✛ ⬭ 3 2 ☰ 1 ✛ 2

Picture That

Use the Directions Box to create a lunar pictograph. Then stu
the graph to answer the questions below.

Directions Box	⭕ = 2 moons
• Draw 2 red moons for Mars. • Draw 15 green moons for Uranus. • Add 1 blue moon for Pluto. • Draw 23 orange moons for Saturn.	• Add 1 gray moon for Earth. • Draw 16 yellow moons for Jupiter. • Add 2 purple moons for Neptune. • There are no moons for Mercury and Venus.

Moons of Our Solar System	
Planet	**Number of Moons**
Mercury	
Venus	
Earth	
Mars	
Jupiter	
Saturn	
Uranus	
Neptune	
Pluto	

1. How many more moons does Saturn have than Uranus?___

2. How many moons do Jupiter, Neptune, and Saturn have altogether? _____

3. Which two planets together have 31 moons? _____

4. Name the planets that have an even number of moons.

_____

low the directions to construct the graph below. Then
the information on the graph to show how many
zas Peppy delivered last year.

ections for constructing the graph:

Write the month abbreviations on the horizontal axis.

Place a title on the top line.

On the vertical axis, write even numbers, counting by 2s.

Plot each point for the number of pizzas sold per month.

Jan.–8	April–17	July–16	Oct.–19
Feb.–15	May–20	Aug.–11	Nov.–22
Mar.–12	June–14	Sept.–9	Dec.–6

Complete the graph by connecting points to show the
change in the deliveries by month.

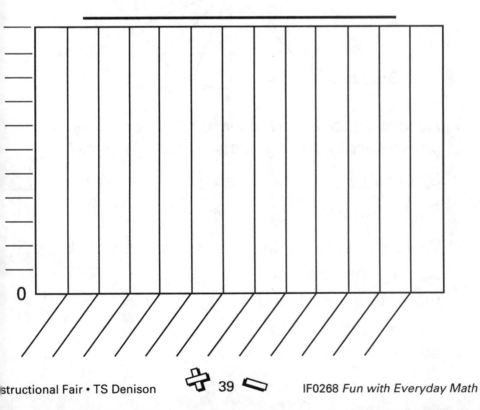

A Piece of the Action

Follow the directions in the box to complete the circle graph. Use your knowledge of fractions to read the gra, and answer the questions below.

Color the sections of the circle graph as shown.
Science—*blue*   English—*green*
Social Studies—*red*   Math—*orange*
Writing—*yellow*

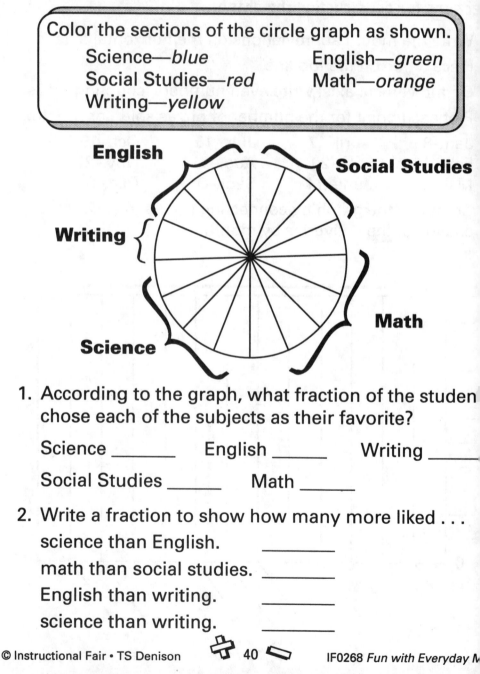

1. According to the graph, what fraction of the studen chose each of the subjects as their favorite?

   Science _____   English _____   Writing _____

   Social Studies _____   Math _____

2. Write a fraction to show how many more liked . . .
   science than English.   _____
   math than social studies.   _____
   English than writing.   _____
   science than writing.   _____

ollow the directions to complete the graph. Then use
at information to answer the questions below.

irections for completing the graph:

Shade vertical colored bars on the graph to show
favorite attractions at the Amusement Park. Label
each axis appropriately.

20	Roller Coaster—*red*	15	Demon Drop—*yellow*
17	Water rides—*blue*	4	Ferris Wheel—*green*
6	Dodge 'Em Cars—*purple*		

Title the graph.

1. What is the difference between the top choice and the lowest choice? _____

2. How many more chose Demon Drop than Dodge 'Em Cars? _____

3. What is the least popular attraction? _____

Fraction Fundamentals

Show your knowledge of fractions. Color each shape according to the directions in each box.

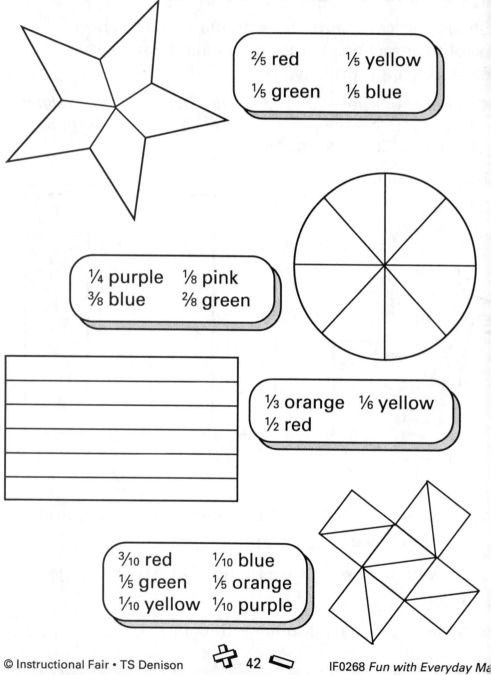

²⁄₅ red	⅕ yellow
⅕ green	⅕ blue

¼ purple	⅛ pink
⅜ blue	²⁄₈ green

⅓ orange	⅙ yellow
½ red	

³⁄₁₀ red	¹⁄₁₀ blue
⅕ green	⅕ orange
¹⁄₁₀ yellow	¹⁄₁₀ purple

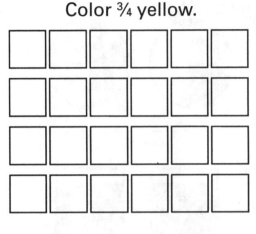
lor each fractional part as directed and complete the
imber sentences.

Color ⅘ yellow.

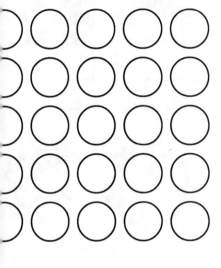

of 25 = _____

Color ¾ yellow.

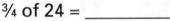

¾ of 24 = _____

Color ⅞ purple.

⅞ of 27 = _____

Color ⅔
blue.

of 24 = _____

Same But Different

Write a number sentence to show the equivalent fraction
pictured.

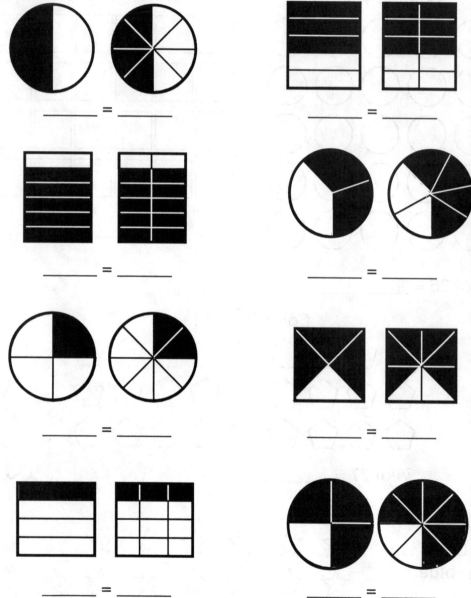

_____ = _____

_____ = _____

_____ = _____

_____ = _____

_____ = _____

_____ = _____

_____ = _____

_____ = _____

...termine the missing numerators. Then write the letters ...the corresponding answers on the lines below to solve ...e riddle.

A
1. $\dfrac{1}{2} = \dfrac{}{10}$

O
2. $\dfrac{3}{5} = \dfrac{}{30}$

U
3. $\dfrac{1}{3} = \dfrac{}{9}$

I
4. $\dfrac{1}{2} = \dfrac{}{28}$

R
5. $\dfrac{3}{8} = \dfrac{}{16}$

N
6. $\dfrac{8}{15} = \dfrac{}{30}$

B
7. $\dfrac{1}{3} = \dfrac{}{21}$

C
8. $\dfrac{2}{5} = \dfrac{}{20}$

S
9. $\dfrac{4}{9} = \dfrac{}{27}$

I
10. $\dfrac{2}{7} = \dfrac{}{14}$

T
11. $\dfrac{5}{8} = \dfrac{}{24}$

T
12. $\dfrac{3}{6} = \dfrac{}{18}$

N
13. $\dfrac{4}{5} = \dfrac{}{20}$

Where should you put mathematicians with back problems?

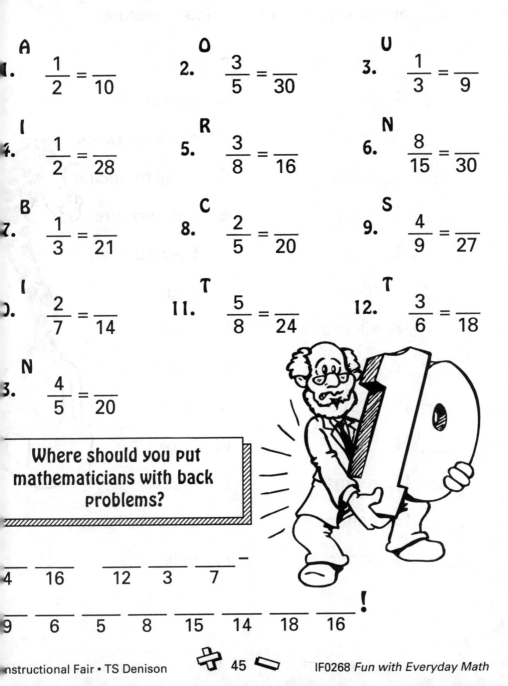

$\overline{}$ $\overline{}$ $\overline{}$ $\overline{}$ $\overline{}$ $-$
4   16   12   3   7

$\overline{}$ $\overline{}$ $\overline{}$ $\overline{}$ $\overline{}$ $\overline{}$ $\overline{}$ $\overline{}$!
9   6   5   8   15   14   18   16

Measure Up

Show which unit of measurement is usually used to measure these common items and events by writing the letter of each item next to the appropriate measure.

____	1. pounds	a.	fruit
____	2. seconds	b.	gravel
____	3. feet	c.	distance races
____	4. yards	d.	baby medicine
____	5. acres	e.	temperature
____	6. degrees	f.	50-yard dash
____	7. tons	g.	eggs
____	8. kilometers	h.	land
____	9. bushels	i.	paper
____	10. drops	j.	fabric
____	11. dozen	k.	books
____	12. reams	l.	meat
____	13. gallons	m.	person's height
____	14. pages	n.	milk

se a centimeter ruler to take a trip through this
aginary constellation cluster. Measure from the
nter of each star.

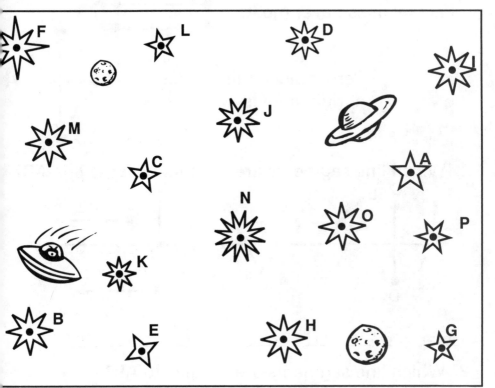

w many centimeters is it from . . . (to nearest cm)

1. C to N   ___ cm   **7.** O to K   ___ cm

2. M to G   ___ cm   **8.** D to H   ___ cm

3. B to H   ___ cm   **9.** E to N   ___ cm

4. L to F   ___ cm   **10.** F to G   ___ cm

5. K to G   ___ cm   **11.** I to J   ___ cm

6. J to M   ___ cm   **12.** K to M   ___ cm

Lines and Angles

Use the information below to answer the questions.

Parallel lines never meet.

Perpendicular lines meet
at right angles.

1. Which line segments are perpendicular to line AB?

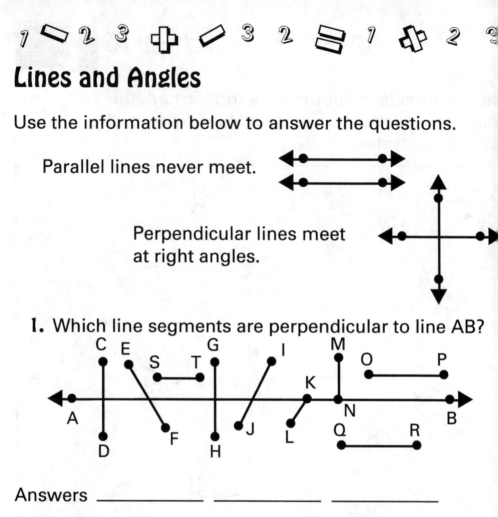

Answers _____ _____ _____

2. Which line segments are parallel to AB?

_____ _____ _____

3. On the alphabet below, draw a red circle around the
letters that have parallel line segments. Then draw a
blue box around letters with perpendicular line
segments.

A B C D E F G H I J
K L M N O P Q R S T
U V W X Y Z

Name the type of angle using the abbreviations O, A, or R. Then name the vertex.

O = obtuse angles 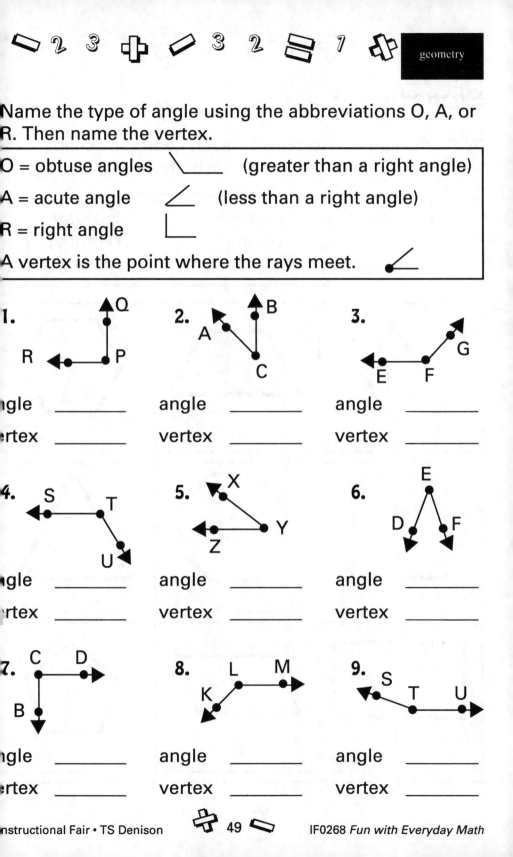 (greater than a right angle)

A = acute angle (less than a right angle)

R = right angle

A vertex is the point where the rays meet.

1.

Q
R P

angle _____
vertex _____

2.

A B
C

angle _____
vertex _____

3.

G
E F

angle _____
vertex _____

4.

S T
U

angle _____
vertex _____

5.

X
Z Y

angle _____
vertex _____

6.

E
D F

angle _____
vertex _____

7.

C D
B

angle _____
vertex _____

8.

L M
K

angle _____
vertex _____

9.

S
T U

angle _____
vertex _____

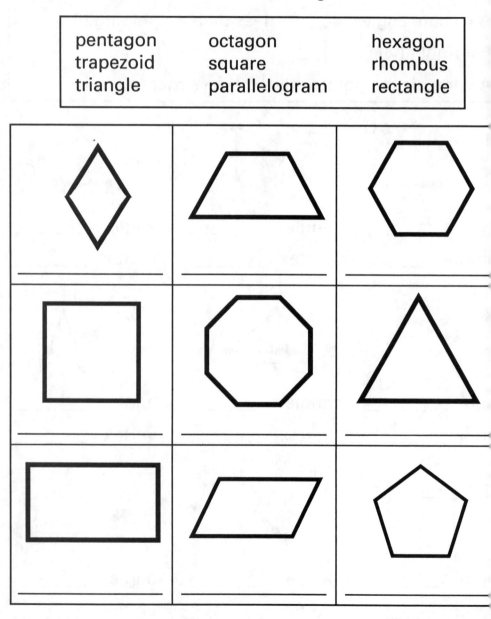

Shape Up

Write the correct word under each geometric shape. The
tell the number of vertices in each figure.

pentagon	octagon	hexagon
trapezoid	square	rhombus
triangle	parallelogram	rectangle

geometry

se the information on each figure to complete the ntence.

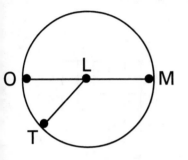

1. The center is at point ____ .
Segment ____ is the diameter.
The radii are ____ , ____ , and ____ .

2. The center is at ____ .
Segment ____ is the diameter.
Segments ____ , ____ , and ____ are the radii.

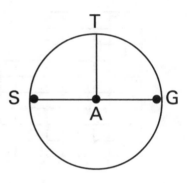

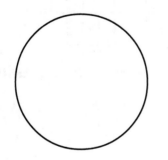

3. Draw a center point and label it **M**. Draw and label an east-west diameter. Then draw and label 2 radii that are at right angles to the diameter.

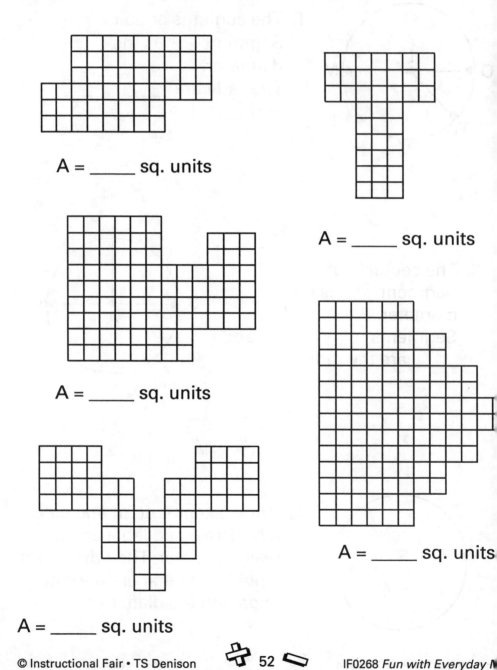

In and Around

Measure these carpet remnants in square units to determine the correct number of units.

A = _____ sq. units

A = _____ sq. units

A = _____ sq. units

A = _____ sq. units

A = _____ sq. units

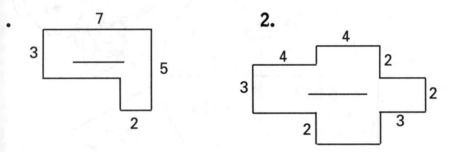
rite the perimeter of each room diagram on the line
side the drawing. The measurements are in feet.

.

7

3

5

2

2.

4

4

3

2

2

2

3

.

2

2

6

1

2

2

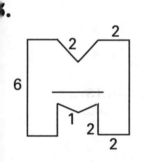

4.

3

1

4

4

14

5.

6

2

1

4

2

6

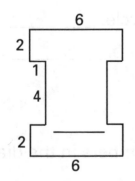

6.

8

2

3

10

1

2

2

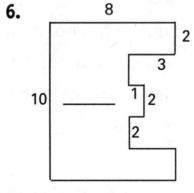

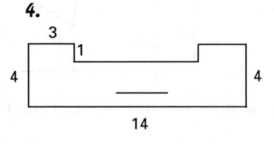

Look Carefully

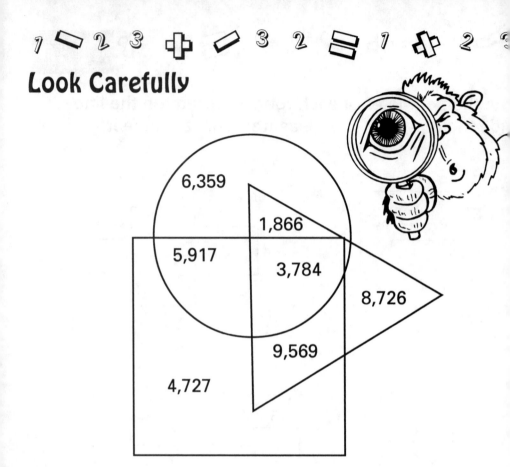

Use scrap paper if needed to add the numbers...

1. in the circle. _____

2. in the square. _____

3. in the square, but not in the triangle. _____

4. in the triangle, but not in the circle. _____

5. in the circle, but not in the square. _____

6. in the triangle. _____

Bonus

What is the grand total of all the numbers in the diagram

_____

your geo-nomics skills. Use the prices listed on each
ape to determine the worth of each configuration.

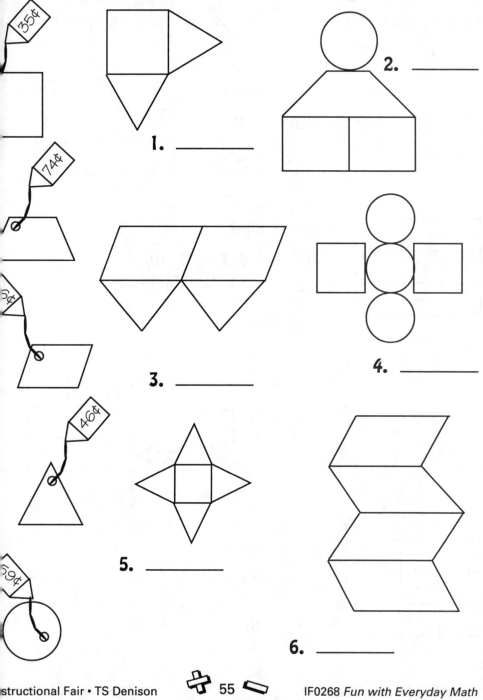

1. _____

2. _____

3. _____

4. _____

5. _____

6. _____

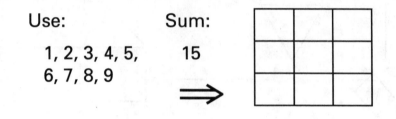

Name That Number

Use the given numbers and arrange them in the squares so that each row ↔ ↕ ↗ equals the sum listed.

Use:

1, 2, 3, 4, 5,
6, 7, 8, 9

Sum:

15

⟹

Sum:

30

⟸

Use:

6, 7, 8, 9, 10,
11, 12, 13, 14

Use:

7, 8, 9, 10, 11
12, 13, 14, 15

Sum:

33

⟹

Sum:

234

⟸

Use:

74, 75, 76, 77,
78, 79, 80, 81,
82

 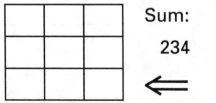

ill in the ▢ s with the numbers 1, 2, 3, 4, 5 so that each
raight line will equal 30. Use each digit only once.

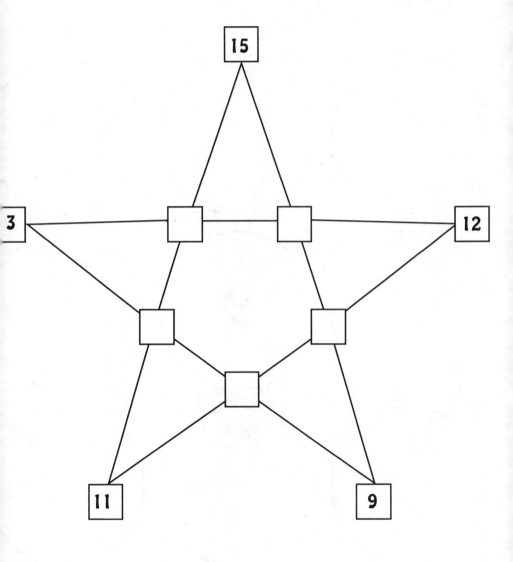

Add 'Em Up

List the odd numbers 1–17. Place these numbers in the circles so that they total 27 in all directions (→ ↓ ← ↗ ↘↑)

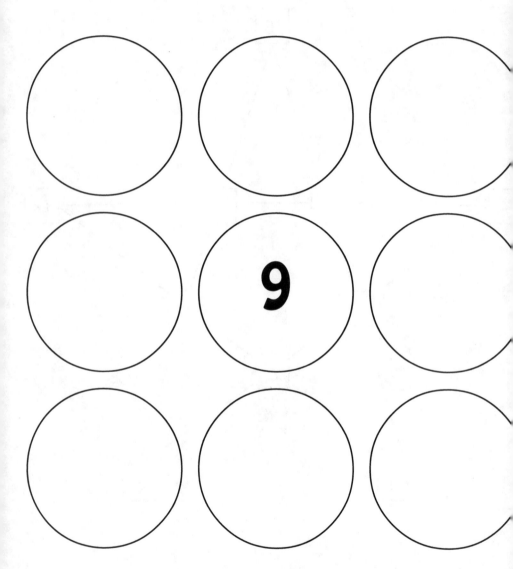

rrange the numbers 1–9 in the triangles to get a sum of
on all 3 sides.

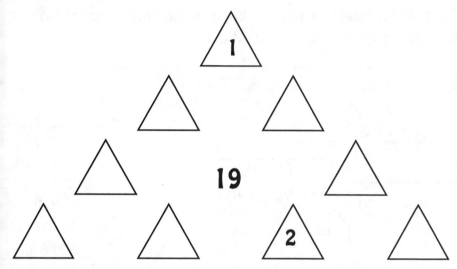

range the numbers 1–9 in the triangles to equal a sum
23 on all 3 sides.

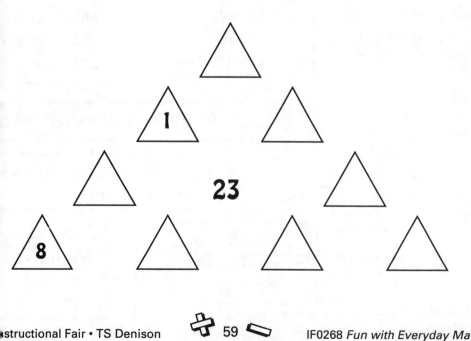

Path Finders

This chain reaction is one continuous math problem. Write the number described and follow the operation in each box to arrive at the final answer.

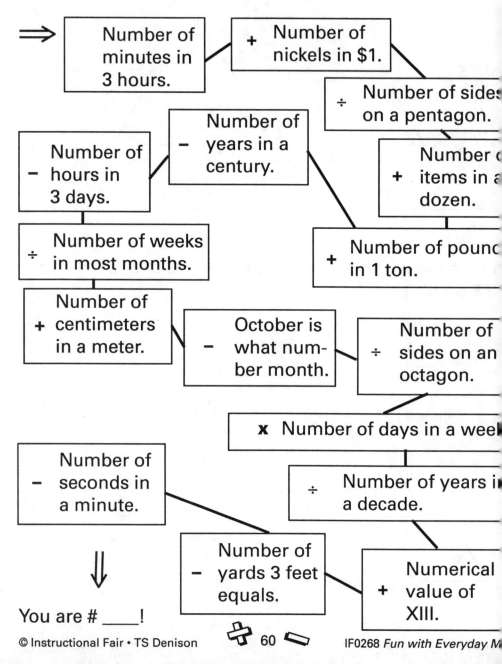

⟹ Number of minutes in 3 hours.

+ Number of nickels in $1.

÷ Number of sides on a pentagon.

Number of years in a century.

− Number of hours in 3 days.

+ Number of items in a dozen.

÷ Number of weeks in most months.

+ Number of pounds in 1 ton.

+ Number of centimeters in a meter.

− October is what number month.

÷ Number of sides on an octagon.

x Number of days in a week.

− Number of seconds in a minute.

÷ Number of years in a decade.

− Number of yards 3 feet equals.

+ Numerical value of XIII.

⟱

You are # ____!

60

ange the numbers 1–13 in the circles so that each row
s a sum of **27**.

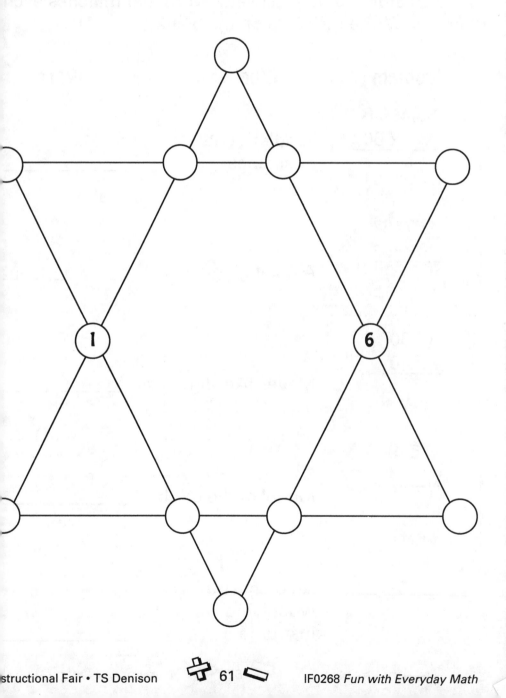

Numbers to Words

Solve each number problem on a calculator. Then turn the calculator 180° to discover a word that matches each definition. Write the word on the blank.

Problem	Clue	Word
1. 83,466.8 <u>x 60</u>	Toddler's cuts or scrapes =	_____
2. 167 167 <u>x 2</u>	A quiet giggle =	_____
3. 1,330 <u>x 40</u>	Moves like slime =	_____
4. 9,519 <u>x 4</u>	Model of the earth =	_____
5. 616 <u>x 5</u>	An orchestra woodwind instrument =	_____

olve each number problem on a calculator. Then turn the
lculator 180° to discover the word that matches each
finition. Write the word on the blank line.

Problem	Clue	Word
1. 63,761.2 _____×5	Turkey's talk =	_____
2. 115,469 _____×5	Homes for some animals =	_____
3. 186,107.5 _____×2	Sound of frying bacon =	_____
4. 896,101 _____×6	Underwater eyegear =	_____
5. 18,455 _____×25	Horse-drawn buggy =	_____

Friends, Romans . . .

Write the Roman numerals for . . .

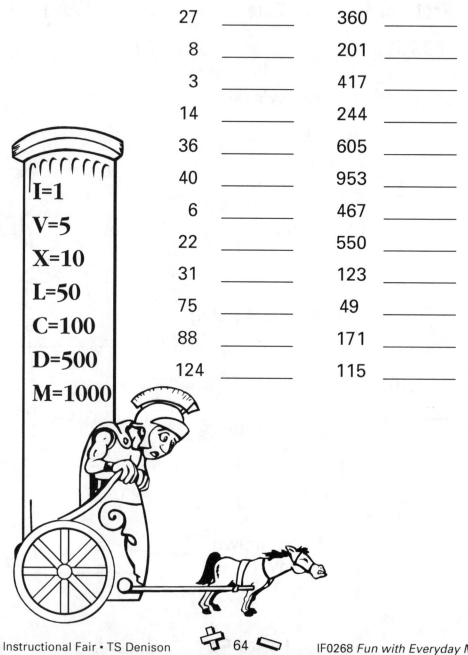

I=1
V=5
X=10
L=50
C=100
D=500
M=1000

27	_____	360	_____
8	_____	201	_____
3	_____	417	_____
14	_____	244	_____
36	_____	605	_____
40	_____	953	_____
6	_____	467	_____
22	_____	550	_____
31	_____	123	_____
75	_____	49	_____
88	_____	171	_____
124	_____	115	_____

'rite the standard numbers for the Roman numerals
;ted below.

LVII _____

DCXXXIV _____

CCCLXXII _____

XVII _____

DCCCLXV _____

CLII _____

MXLII _____

DCCXLVI _____

CXII _____

LIX _____

DCCL _____

DCCCXLIII _____

XXIX _____

CMXXII _____

CCII _____

LXVI _____

CCCLXXXIV _____

CMXIX _____

LXXIX _____

CLXII _____

I=1

V=5

X=10

L=50

C=100

D=500

M=1000

Units of Measure

Give the volume for each of these shapes. Volume is the number of cubic units in a 3-dimensional object.

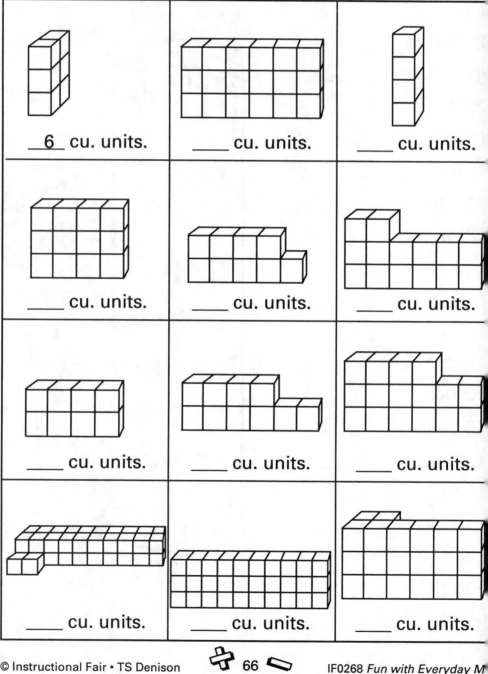

__6__ cu. units.

____ cu. units.

____ cu. units.

____ cu. units.

____ cu. units.

____ cu. units.

____ cu. units.

____ cu. units.

____ cu. units.

____ cu. units.

____ cu. units.

____ cu. units.

e an inch ruler and follow the directions to create a
:ture in the box.

1. Draw a 1½" tall x 4" wide rectangle in the lower half of the box.

2. Place 3–1" squares equally spaced atop the rectangle.

3. Draw a red cone, a yellow cone, and a blue cone atop each square.

4. Now add matching flags above each cone shape.

5. Place a 2" wide x 1" high arched door at the center of the bottom of the rectangle.

6. Divide the door into two halves with a vertical line.

7. Add additional details to this medieval structure.

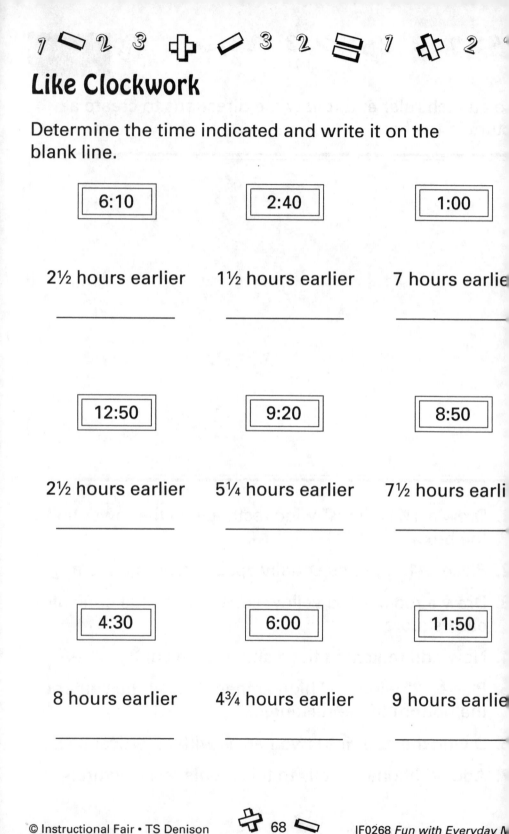
Like Clockwork

Determine the time indicated and write it on the
blank line.

| 6:10 | 2:40 | 1:00 |

2½ hours earlier   1½ hours earlier   7 hours earlie

_____   _____   _____

| 12:50 | 9:20 | 8:50 |

2½ hours earlier   5¼ hours earlier   7½ hours earli

_____   _____   _____

| 4:30 | 6:00 | 11:50 |

8 hours earlier   4¾ hours earlier   9 hours earlie

_____   _____   _____

termine the elapsed time as indicated and write it on
line.

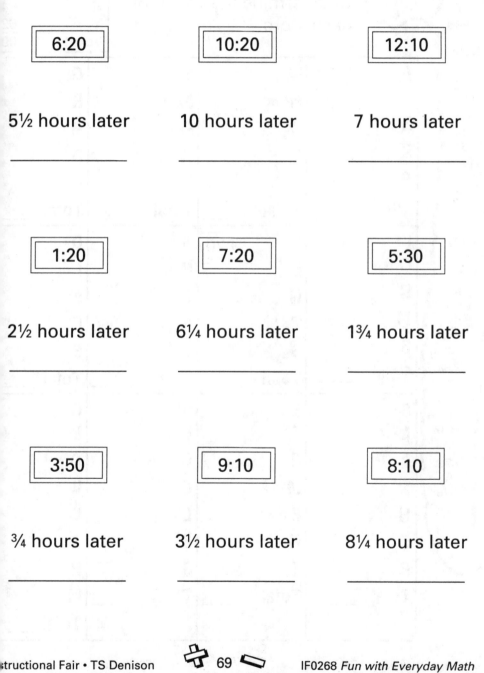

6:20

5½ hours later

_____

10:20

10 hours later

_____

12:10

7 hours later

_____

1:20

2½ hours later

_____

7:20

6¼ hours later

_____

5:30

1¾ hours later

_____

3:50

¾ hours later

_____

9:10

3½ hours later

_____

8:10

8¼ hours later

_____

Sum Fun with Computation

Use a calculator and the prices on Willie Worthmore to determine the worth of each word.

Example:	
M	$3.43
O	1.55
N	4.76
E	2.64
Y	.62
Total	**$13.00**

Willie Worthmore:

- Z $1.47
- T $0.84
- S $2.19
- R $1.85
- P $0.66
- O $1.55
- N $4.76
- M $3.43
- L $0.77
- I $2.29
- H $3.58
- G $0.89
- E $2.64
- D $1.67
- C $2.37
- F $1.75
- A $1.15
- W $0.68
- Y $0.62

P I Z Z A Total ___	W H A L E Total ___	S M A R T Total ___	G R A D E Total ___
W O R M S Total ___	C E N T S Total ___	S P E N D Total ___	D I M E S Total ___
S L I T H E R Total ___	S E G M E N T Total ___	W I G G L E S Total ___	G L O W W O R M Total ___

IF0268 *Fun with Everyday M*

hen added together, the mystery numbers equal the sum
ven. When the same two numbers are multiplied, they
ual the quotient given. Write the mystery numbers in the
xes.

1.
? + ? = 15
? x ? = 56
☐ , ☐

2.
? + ? = 18
? x ? = 81
☐ , ☐

3.
? + ? = 10
? x ? = 24
☐ , ☐

4.
? + ? = 13
? x ? = 36
☐ , ☐

5.
? + ? = 8
? x ? = 15
☐ , ☐

6.
? + ? = 12
? x ? = 32
☐ , ☐

7.
? + ? = 12
? x ? = 35
☐ , ☐

8.
? + ? = 8
? x ? = 16
☐ , ☐

9.
? + ? = 16
? x ? = 63
☐ , ☐

10.
? + ? = 13
? x ? = 42
☐ , ☐

11.
? + ? = 15
? x ? = 54
☐ , ☐

12.
? + ? = 16
? x ? = 64
☐ , ☐

13.
? + ? = 11
? x ? = 18
☐ , ☐

14.
? + ? = 12
? x ? = 36
☐ , ☐

15.
? + ? = 17
? x ? = 72
☐ , ☐

Don't Get Mixed Up

Write each fraction as a whole number or mixed number in the lowest terms.

1.
$$\frac{9}{6} =$$

2.
$$\frac{10}{4} =$$

3.
$$\frac{14}{6} =$$

4.
$$\frac{12}{4} =$$

5.
$$\frac{21}{9} =$$

6.
$$\frac{8}{6} =$$

7.
$$\frac{18}{8} =$$

8.
$$\frac{12}{10} =$$

9.
$$\frac{15}{3} =$$

10.
$$\frac{12}{8} =$$

11.
$$\frac{20}{6} =$$

12.
$$\frac{13}{6} =$$

13.
$$\frac{24}{12} =$$

14.
$$\frac{10}{8} =$$

15.
$$\frac{9}{2} =$$